The

This i ....

Copyright © 2010
by
David E. Robinson

All Rights Reserved
Parts of this book may be reproduced subject to due
and specific acknowledgment of their source.

MAINE-PATRIOT.com
3 Linnell Circle
Brunswick, Maine 04011

maine-patriot.com

The Road Ahead

Contents

The Road Ahead ---------------- 5
About Sarah --------------------------- 7
1 Gov. Sarah Louise Palin -------------- 9
2 Gov. Palin on Environment ----------- 39
3 Highlights of 'Going Rogue' ---------- 45

New Kid On The Block --------- 79
4 Gov. Elect Debra Medina ------------ 81
5 Debra Medina On Issues ------------ 87

9/11 Truther Controversy ----- 93
6 Sarah Palin:
   On Investigating 9/11 --------- 95
7 Debra Medina:
   On Investigating 9/11 --------- 97

8 9/11 Truth Movement ----------------- 103

Debra Medina On The Home -113
9 The Home ---------------------------- 115

Born Again, American --------- 121

This is Woman's Hour

"I appealed to your best hopes...."

"Whatever else history may say about me when I'm gone, I hope it will record that I appealed to your best hopes, not your worst fears: to your confidence rather than your doubts. My dream is that you will travel the road ahead with liberty's lamp guiding your steps and opportunity's arm steadying your way."

— President Ronald Reagan, 1992

THE ROAD AHEAD

This is Woman's Hour

ABOUT SARAH

Governor Sarah Palin first made history on Dec. 4, 2006. Sworn in that day as the 11th governor of Alaska, she is the first woman to hold the office. In August 2008, Senator John McCain tapped Governor Palin to serve as his vice presidential running mate in his Presidential campaign, thus making her the first woman to run on the Republican Party's presidential ticket.

In Alaska, her top priorities have been resource development, education, health, and transportation and infrastructure development. Governor Palin has fought for reform and transparency in government.

Governor Palin has a long record of achievement and experience in public office. Prior to her election as governor, Palin served two terms on the Wasilla City Council and two terms as the mayor/manager of Wasilla. During her tenure, she reduced property tax levels while increasing services and made Wasilla a business friendly environment, drawing in new industry.

Under her leadership as Governor, Alaska has invested $5 billion in state savings, overhauled education funding, and implemented the Senior Benefits Program that provides support for low-income older Alaskans. She created Alaska's Petroleum Systems Integrity Office to provide oversight and maintenance of oil and gas equipment, facilities and infrastructure, and the Climate Change Subcabinet to prepare a climate change strategy for Alaska.

During her first legislative session, Governor Palin's administration passed two major pieces of legislation - an overhaul of the state's ethics laws and a competitive process to construct a gas pipeline.

Governor Palin is past chair of the Interstate Oil and Gas Compact Commission, a multi-state government agency that promotes the conservation and efficient recovery of domestic oil and natural gas resources while protecting health, safety and the environment. She was recently named chair of the National Governors Association (NGA) Natural Resources Committee, which is charged with pursuing legislation to ensure state needs are considered as federal policy is formulated in the areas of agriculture, energy, environmental protection and natural resource management.

Sarah Heath Palin arrived in Alaska with her family in 1964, when her parents came to teach school in Skagway. She received a Bachelor of Science Degree in Communications-Journalism from the University of Idaho in 1987.

She is married to Todd Palin, who is a lifelong Alaskan, a production operator on the North Slope and a four-time champion of the Iron Dog, the world's longest snow machine race. They have five children.

Gov. Sarah Louise Palin

1
Gov. Sarah Louise Palin

Sarah Louise Palin [Heath]; (*born February 11, 1964*) is an *American* politician who served as *Governor of Alaska* from 2006 until *she stepped down in 2009*. She was the *Republican* candidate for *Vice President of the United States* in 2008.

Sarah was a member of the *Wasilla, Alaska, city council* from 1992 to 1996 and the city's *mayor* from 1996 to 2002. After an unsuccessful campaign for *Lieutenant Governor* of Alaska in 2002, she chaired the *Alaska Oil and Gas Conservation Commission* from 2003 until her resignation in 2004. She was elected *Governor of Alaska* in November 2006. Palin became the first *female governor* of Alaska and the *youngest person* ever elected as governor of that state.

In 2008, Republican presidential candidate *John McCain* chose Sarah as his *running mate* in that year's *presidential election,* making her the *second female candidate* and the *first Alaskan candidate* of either major party on a national ticket, as well as the *first female vice-presidential nominee of the Republican Party*. Since the defeat of the McCain–Palin ticket in the 2008 election, there has been speculation that she may run for the *Republican presidential nomination* in 2012.

On July 3, 2009, Sarah announced she would not seek reelection as governor and that she was stepping down, effective July 26, 2009, eighteen months prior to the completion of her first term. She cited frivolous, *harassing ethics complaints* that had been filed following her selection as running mate to John McCain as the reason for her leaving the office of governor, saying the resulting *fruitless investigations* had affected her efficacy to govern the state.

History, Structure, Mission

The *Alaska Oil and Gas Conservation Commission* (AOGCC) is a *quasi-judicial* agency in the U.S. state of Alaska, within Alaska's *Department of Administration*. The Commission was established in 1955, was subsequently abolished, and eventually reestablished. This Commission is responsible for overseeing oil and gas drilling and production, reservoir depletion, and certain other operations on private and state-owned lands in Alaska.

A territorial statute created the *Alaska Oil and Gas Conservation Commission* (AOGCC) in 1955, before Alaska became a state in 1959. At that time, the Commission comprised the *Territorial Governor, the Commissioner of Mines,* and the *Highway Engineer*. Rules and regulations for the Commission's activities took effect in 1958.

In 1959, the *Oil and Gas Conservation Commission* was temporarily abolished, and its duties were transferred to the *Alaska Department of Natural Resources*. In 1968, the *Division of Oil and Gas* was formed within the *Department of Natural Resources*. In 1976, the word "conservation" was added back to the division's title, and it became the *Division of Oil and Gas Conservation*.

In 1977, with oil production occurring in Prudhoe Bay, the *Alaska Legislature* decided that an independent quasi-judicial agency should be created in the executive branch of the state. The present independent agency was at first located within the *Department of Natural Resources,* but in 1980 was transferred to the *Department of Commerce* and Economic Development. In 1994, it was transferred to the Department of Administration.

The structure of the membership has changed throughout the years, though it has consistently been a *three-member Commission.*

Under the current structure, adopted in 1979, one member must be *a registered petroleum engineer,* one member must be *a registered geologist,* and one member must *represent the public at large* (i.e., a citizen in neither of the two categories listed above).

The Commission is tasked to work *in-hand with the oil industry* to maximize production, administer correlative rights, and improve resource recovery. It also administers an *underground injection program* for enhanced oil recovery and underground disposal of oil field waste, as authorized by the U.S. Environmental Protection Agency. As part of this injection process, *oil corporations must obtain an Aquifer Exemption Order* granted by the AOGCC in areas with deep groundwater supplies. Some environmental groups such as the *Cook Inletkeeper* as well as *First Nation People* have contested these Orders, fearing they may contaminate groundwater supplies. The Commission also holds oversight of wastewater disposal known as *"wastewater drain fields,"* where as such, oil corporations are permitted to dispose of wastewater in the soil when certain requirements are met ; and reject Orders when not met. Additionally, the Commission adjudicates *certain oil and gas disputes* between owners, including *disputes where the state is a party.* It is designed to cooperate with industry, *while still meeting its regulatory requirements.* The Commission's website lists their primary mission is *"to protect the public interest in exploration and development of oil and gas resources, while ensuring conservation practices, enhancing resource recovery, and protecting the health, safety, environment, and property rights of Alaskans."* Although the Cook Inletkeeper website notes that *"2 billion gallons of toxic waste"* are disposed of in the Cook Inlet waterway every year by oil corporations

Early life and career

Palin was born in *Sandpoint, Idaho*, the third of four children born to Sarah and Charles R. Heath, respectively a school secretary and science teacher / track coach. The family moved to Alaska when she was an infant. She attended *Wasilla High School*, where she was the head of the *Fellowship of Christian Athletes*, and a member of the girls' cross country team. As captain and point guard of the school's *girls' basketball team* that won the Alaska state championship in 1982, she gained the nickname *"Barracuda"* for her competitive streak. She graduated in 1982.

She attended *Hawaii Pacific University* in the Fall of 1982 and *North Idaho College* (whose Alumni Association gave her the *Distinguished Alumni Achievement Award* in June 2008) in the Spring and Fall of 1983. In 1984, after winning the *Miss Wasilla pageant,* she finished third in the *Miss Alaska pageant,* receiving the *"Miss Congeniality"* award and a college scholarship.

She attended the *University of Idaho* in the Fall of 1984 and Spring of 1985, *Matanuska-Susitna College* in the Fall of 1985, and the *University of Idaho* again in the Spring and Fall of 1986 and the Fall of 1987, when she received her *Bachelor's degree in communications* with an emphasis in *journalism*.

Palin's early ambition was to be a *sportscaster.* Accordingly, after graduating, she worked as a *sportscaster* for

KTUU-TV and KTVA-TV in Anchorage, and as a *sports reporter* for the *Mat-Su Valley Frontiersman.* In 1988, she eloped with her childhood sweetheart *Todd Palin,* believing that her parents "couldn't afford a big white wedding." After the marriage, she helped in her husband's commercial fishing business.

Early political career
Wasilla city council

Motivated by concerns that revenue from a new *Wasilla sales tax* would not be spent wisely, Palin was elected to the *city council of Wasilla* in 1992. She won 530 (63%) votes to 310. She ran for reelection in 1995, winning by 413 (69%) votes to 185, but did not complete her second term on the city council because she was elected mayor in 1996. Throughout her tenure on the city council and the rest of her career, Palin has been a registered Republican.

Mayor of Wasilla

Palin served two three-year terms (1996–2002) as the mayor of *Wasilla.* In 1996, she defeated three-term incumbent mayor John Stein, on a platform *targeting wasteful spending and high taxes.* Stein says that Palin introduced *abortion, gun rights,* and *term limits* as campaign issues. Although the election was a *nonpartisan blanket primary,* the state Republican Party ran advertisements on her behalf. At the conclusion of Palin's tenure as mayor in 2002, the city had about 6,300 residents. In 2008, Wasilla's mayor credited Palin's tax cuts and infrastructural improvements with helping the local economy, "bringing the big-box stores to Wasilla, ... helping Wasilla grow and draw 50,000 shoppers a day." The *Boston Globe* quoted a local business owner as crediting Palin with making the town "more of a community ... It's no longer a little strip town that you can blow through in a heartbeat."

First term, *Wasilla, Alaska*

Shortly after taking office in October 1996, Palin consolidated the position of museum director and asked for updated *resumes and resignation letters* from "city department heads who had been loyal to Stein," including the police chief, public works director, finance director, and librarian. Palin stated this request was *to find out their intentions and whether they supported her.* She temporarily required department heads *to get her approval before talking to reporters,* saying that they first needed to become acquainted with her administration's policies. She created the position of city administrator, and *reduced her own $68,000 salary* by 10%, although by mid-1998 *this was reversed by the city council.*

During her first year in office, Palin kept a jar with the names of Wasilla residents on her desk. Once a week, she pulled a name from it and picked up the phone; she would ask: "How's the city doing?" Using income generated by a 2% sales tax that was enacted before she was elected to the city council, Palin *cut property taxes by 75%* and eliminated *personal property and business inventory taxes.*[Using municipal bonds, she made improvements to the roads and sewers, and increased funding to the Police Department. She also oversaw *new bike paths* and procured funding for *storm-water treatment* to protect freshwater resources. At the same time, the city reduced spending on the town museum and stopped construction of a new library and city hall.

Palin ran for re-election against Stein in 1999 and won, with 74% of the vote. She was also elected president of the *Alaska Conference of Mayors.*

Palin appointed Charles Fannon to replace Stambaugh as police chief.

Second term

During her second term as mayor, Palin introduced a *ballot measure* proposing the construction of a *municipal sports center* to be financed by a 0.5% sales tax increase. The $14.7 million *Wasilla Multi-Use Sports Complex* was built on time and under budget, but the city spent an additional $1.3 million because of an *eminent domain lawsuit* caused by the failure to obtain clear title to the property before beginning construction. The city's long-term debt grew from about $1 million to $25 million through *voter-approved indebtedness* of $15 million for the sports complex, $5.5 million for street projects, and $3 million for water improvement projects. A city council member defended the spending increases as being *caused by the city's growth* during that time.

Palin also joined with nearby communities in jointly hiring the Anchorage-based lobbying firm of *Robertson, Monagle & Eastaugh* to lobby for federal funds. The firm secured nearly $8 million in *earmarked funds* for the Wasilla city government. Earmarks included $500,000 for a *youth shelter,* $1.9 million for a *transportation hub,* and $900,000 for *sewer repairs.* Term limits in the Wasilla Municipal Code proscribe candidates from running for more than two consecutive terms.

Controversies

Wasilla librarian Mary Ellen Emmons strongly objected to remarks by Palin that Emmons characterized as being about *book censorship.* Emmons said that Palin asked two or three times in October 1996 if she would object to books being removed from the library. Palin has said the question was "rhetorical". John Stein, the former mayor of Wasilla and Palin's 1996 political opponent, said in September 2008 that Palin's *"religious beliefs"* and the concerns of some voters about language in the books, *motivated her inquiries.* In December 1996, Palin said she had no books or other material in mind for removal. No books were removed from the library, and Palin stated in 2006 that she *would not allow her personal religious beliefs* to dictate her political positions.

Police Chief Irl Stambaugh, who was eventually fired by Palin *for due cause* was previously nominated to be Alaska's Municipal Employee of the Year. Because he had heard that Palin had felt intimidated by him during a meeting, he made sure to sit when talking with her, and to use a soothing voice. Nevertheless, Palin said, *"When I met with you in private, instead of engaging in interactive conversation with me, you gave me short, uncommunicative answers and then you would sit there and stare at me in silence with a very stern look, like you were trying to intimidate me."* On January 30, Stambaugh was on the phone with the town's librarian — who said she had just been fired — when an assistant of Palin's walked up and gave Stambaugh an envelope. Inside was a letter from Palin, saying Stambaugh, too, was fired. His firing was to be effective February 13.

Palin said that she fired Emmons and Stambaugh because *they did not fully support her efforts to govern the city.* The next day, following expressions of public support for Emmons at a personal meeting, *Palin rescinded the firing of Emmons,* stating that her concerns had been alleviated, and adding that *Emmons agreed to support Palin's plan to merge the town's library and museum operations.*

Palin described the letters as just a test of loyalty. Stambaugh, who along with Emmons *had supported Palin's opponent in the election,* filed a lawsuit alleging *wrongful termination, violation of his contract,* and *gender discrimination.* In the trial, the defense alleged *political reasons;* Stambaugh said that he had opposed a gun control bill, Alaska Senate Bill 177, that Palin supported. The federal judge said in the decision that *the police chief serves at the discretion of the mayor, and can be terminated for nearly any reason, even a political one,* and dismissed Stambaugh's lawsuit ordering Stambaugh to pay Palin's legal fees.

Post-mayoral years

In 2002, Palin ran for the Republican nomination for *lieutenant governor,* coming in *second* to Loren Leman in a five-way Republican primary. The Republican ticket of U.S. Senator Frank Murkowski and Leman won the November 2002 election. When Murkowski resigned from his long-held *U.S. Senate seat* in December 2002 to become governor, he *considered* appointing Palin to replace him in the Senate, but chose his daughter, *State Representative Lisa Murkowski instead.*

Governor Murkowski appointed Palin to the *Alaska Oil and Gas Conservation Commission.* She chaired the Commission beginning in 2003, serving as *Ethics Supervisor.* Palin resigned in January 2004, protesting what she called the *"lack of ethics" of fellow Republican members.*

After resigning, Palin *filed a formal complaint against Oil and Gas Conservation Commissioner Randy Ruedrich,* also the chair of the state Republican Party, *accusing him of doing work for the party on public time and of working closely with a company he was supposed to be regulat-*

ing. She also joined with Democratic legislator Eric Croft to file a complaint against Gregg Renkes, *a former Alaskan Attorney General,* accusing him of *having a financial conflict of interest in negotiating a coal exporting trade agreement, while Renkes was the subject of investigation and after records suggesting a possible conflict of interest had been released to the public.* Ruedrich and Renkes both resigned and Ruedrich paid a record $12,000 fine.

From 2003 to June 2005, Palin served as *one of three directors* of *"Ted Stevens Excellence in Public Service, Inc.,"* a *527 group* designed to provide political training for Republican women in Alaska. In 2004, Palin told the *Anchorage Daily News* that she had decided not to run for the U.S. Senate that year, against the Republican incumbent, *Lisa Murkowski,* because her teenage son opposed it. Palin said, *"How could I be the team mom if I was a U.S. Senator?"*

Governor of Alaska

In 2006, running on a clean-government platform, Palin defeated *incumbent Governor Frank Murkowski* in the *Republican gubernatorial primary.* Her running mate was *State Senator Sean Parnell.* She will not be a candidate for re-election as Governor in 2010.

In the November election, Palin was *outspent but victorious,* defeating former Democratic governor Tony Knowles by a margin of 48.3% to 40.9%. She became *Alaska's first female governor,* at the age of 42, the youngest governor in Alaskan history, the state's first governor to have been born after Alaska achieved U.S. statehood, *and the first not to be inaugurated in the state capital Juneau* (*she chose to have the ceremony held in Fairbanks instead*).

She took office on December 4, 2006, and for most of

her term was very popular with Alaska voters. Polls taken in 2007 showed her with 93% and 89% popularity among all voters, which led *some media outlets* to call her *"the most popular governor in America."* A poll taken in late September 2008 after Palin was named to the national Republican ticket showed her popularity in Alaska at 68%. A poll taken in May 2009 showed Palin's popularity among Alaskans was at 54% positive and 41.6% negative.

Palin declared that top priorities of her administration would be *resource development, education and workforce development, public health and safety,* and *transportation and infrastructure development.* She had championed *ethics reform* throughout her election campaign. Her first legislative action after taking office was to *push for a bipartisan ethics reform bill.* She signed the resulting legislation in July 2007, calling it a "first step" *declaring that she remained determined to clean up Alaska politics.*

Palin has frequently *broken with the state Republican establishment.* For example, she endorsed Sean Parnell's bid to unseat the state's longtime at-large U.S. Representative, Don Young, and she publicly challenged then-Senator Ted Stevens *to come clean about the federal investigation into his financial dealings.* Shortly before his July 2008 indictment, she held a joint news conference with Stevens, described by *The Washington Post* as needed "to make clear she had not abandoned him politically."

Palin promoted *oil and natural gas resource development in Alaska, including drilling in the Arctic National Wildlife Refuge* (ANWR). Proposals to drill for oil in ANWR have been the subject of a *national debate.*

In 2006, Palin obtained a passport and in 2007 traveled for the first time outside of North America on a trip to Kuwait. There she visited the *Khabari Alawazem Crossing* at the Kuwait–Iraq border and met with members of the *Alaska National Guard* at several bases.[On her return trip to the U.S., *she visited injured soldiers in Germany.*

Budget, spending, and federal funds

In June 2007, Palin signed *a record $6.6 billion operating budget into law.* At the same time, she used her veto power to *make the second-largest cuts of the construction budget in state history.* The $237 million in cuts represented over 300 local projects, and *reduced the construction budget to $1.6 billion.* In 2008, Palin vetoed $286 million, *cutting or reducing funding for 350 projects* from the FY09 capital budget.

Palin followed through on a campaign promise *to sell the Westwind II jet, a purchase made by the Murkowski administration for $2.7 million in 2005 against the wishes of the legislature.* In August 2007, the jet was listed on eBay, but the sale fell through, and the plane *was later sold for $2.1 million through a private brokerage firm.*

Gubernatorial expenditures

Palin lived in Juneau during the legislative session and lived in Wasilla and worked out of offices in Anchorage the rest of the year. Since the office in Anchorage is far from Juneau, *while she worked there, state officials said she was permitted to claim a $58 per diem travel allowance, which she took* (a total of $16,951), *and reimbursements for hotels, which she refused,* choosing to drive 50 miles to her home in Wasilla instead. *She also chose not to use the former governor's private chef.*

Republicans and Democrats criticized Palin for taking the *per diem* and $43,490 in travel expenses for when her family accompanied her on state business. In response, the governor's staffers said that *these practices were in line with state policy,* that Palin's gubernatorial expenses *were 80% below those of her predecessor,* Frank Murkowski, and that *"many of the hundreds of invitations Palin receives include requests for her to bring her family, placing the definition of 'state business' with the party extending the invitation."*

In February 2009, the State of Alaska, *reversing a policy that had treated the payments as legitimate business expenses under the Internal Revenue Code,* decided that per diems paid to state employees for stays in their own homes will be treated as taxable income and will be included in employees' gross income on their W-2 forms. *Palin herself had ordered the review of the tax policy.*

In December 2008, an *Alaska State Commission* recommended increasing the Governor's annual salary from $125,000 to $150,000. *Palin stated that she would not accept the pay raise.* In response, the commission dropped the recommendation.

Federal funding

In her *State of the State Address* on January 17, 2008, Palin declared that *the people of Alaska "can and must continue to develop our economy, because we cannot and must not rely so heavily on federal government [funding]."* Alaska's federal congressional representatives cut back on *pork-barrel project requests* during Palin's time as governor; despite this, in 2008 *Alaska was still the largest per-capita recipient of federal earmarks,* requesting nearly $750 million in special federal spending over a period of two years.

While there is no sales tax or income tax in Alaska, *state revenues doubled to $10 billion in 2008.* For the 2009 budget, Palin gave a list of 31 proposed federal earmarks or requests for funding, totaling $197 million, to Alaska Senator Ted Stevens. *Palin's decreasing support for federal funding has been a leading source of friction between herself and the state's congressional delegation;* Palin has requested less in federal funding each year than her predecessor Frank Murkowski requested in his last year.

Bridge to Nowhere, *Gravina Island Bridge*

In 2005, before Palin was elected governor, Congress passed a *$442-million earmark* for constructing *two Alaska bridges* as part of an omnibus spending bill. The Gravina Island Bridge received nationwide attention as a symbol of *pork-barrel spending,* following news reports that the bridge would cost $233 million in Federal funds. Because *Gravina Island, the site of the Ketchikan airport,* has a population of 50, *the bridge became known nationally as the "Bridge to Nowhere".* Following an outcry by the public and some members of the US Senate, *Congress eliminated the bridge earmark* from the spending bill but *gave the allotted funds to Alaska as part of its general transportation fund.*

In 2006, Palin ran for governor with a *"build-the-bridge" plank* in her platform, saying she would "not allow the spinmeisters to turn this project ... into something that's so negative." Palin criticized the use of the word "nowhere" as *insulting to local residents* and urged speedy work on building the infrastructure *"while our congressional delegation is in a strong position to assist."*

As governor, Palin *canceled the Gravina Island Bridge* in September 2007, saying that Congress had *"little interest in spending any more money"* due to what she called *"inaccurate portrayals of the projects."* Alaska chose not to return the $442 million in federal transportation funds.

In 2008, as a vice-presidential candidate, *Palin characterized her position as having told Congress "thanks, but no thanks, on that bridge to nowhere."* This angered some Alaskans in Ketchikan, who said that the claim was false and a betrayal of Palin's previous support for their community. Some critics complained that this statement was misleading, since she had expressed support for the spending project and kept the Federal money after the project was canceled. *Palin received criticism for allowing construction of a 3-mile access road, built with $25 million in Federal transportation funds set aside as part of the original bridge project, to continue.* A spokesman for Alaska's Department of Transportation made a statement that it was within Palin's power to cancel the road project, but also noted that the state was still considering cheaper designs to complete the bridge project, and that in any case the road would open up the surrounding lands for development.

Gas pipeline

The Alaska gas pipeline is a proposal to transport natural gas from the <u>Alaska North Slope</u> *natural gas reserves* to the U.S. Midwest via Chicago. There are two competing projects: *one by BP and ConocoPhillips* called "Denali", and *another by* <u>TransCanada Corp.</u> *and* <u>ExxonMobil</u>. TransCanada has secured state seed money and a license from the state of Alaska to build and operate a pipeline, but does not yet have federal approvals needed to start construction. Denali is spending its own money to move the project forward. Both entities have said they plan to hold their respective *"open seasons"* in 2010. On June 11, 2009 TransCanada announced it had formed an agreement with

ExxonMobil to work together in bringing the gas to market.

In August 2008, Palin signed a bill authorizing the State of Alaska to award *TransCanada Pipelines*—the sole bidder to meet the state's requirements—a license to build and operate a pipeline to transport natural gas from *Alaska's North Slope* to the *Continental United States* through *Canada.* The governor also pledged $500 million in seed money to support the project. It is estimated that the project will cost $26 billion. *Newsweek* described the project as *"the principal achievement of Sarah Palin's term as Alaska's governor."* The pipeline faces legal challenges from Canadian *First Nations.*

Predator control

In 2007, Palin supported a 2003 *Alaska Department of Fish and Game* policy allowing the *hunting of wolves from the air* as part of a predator control program intended to *increase moose and caribou populations for subsistence-food gatherers and other hunters.* In March 2007, Palin's office announced that a *bounty of $150 per wolf would be paid to the 180 volunteer pilots and gunners, to offset fuel costs, in five areas of Alaska.* Six-hundred-and-seven wolves had been killed in the prior four years. State biologists wanted 382 to 664 wolves killed by the end of the predator-control season in April 2007. Wildlife activists sued the state, *and a state judge declared the bounty illegal* on the basis that a bounty would have to be offered by the Board of Game and not by the Department of Fish and Game.

Public Safety Commissioner dismissal

Palin dismissed Public Safety Commissioner Walt Monegan on July 11, 2008, citing *performance-related issues, such as not being "a team player on budgeting is-*

sues" and "egregious rogue behavior." Palin attorney Van Flein said that the "last straw" was Monegan's *planned trip to Washington, D.C., to seek funding for a new, multimillion-dollar sexual assault initiative* the governor hadn't yet approved. Monegan said that he had resisted persistent pressure from the Governor, her husband, and her staff, including State Attorney General Talis Colberg, *to fire Palin's ex-brother-in-law, state trooper Mike Wooten;* Wooten was involved in a child custody battle with Palin's sister after a bitter divorce that included *an alleged death threat against Palin's father*. At one point Sarah and Todd Palin hired a private investigator to get Wooten disciplined. Monegan stated that he learned *an internal investigation had found all but two of the allegations to be unsubstantiated,* and Wooten had been disciplined for the others—*an illegal moose killing and the tasering of an 11-year-old* (the child asked to be Tasered?). He told the Palins that there was nothing he could do because the matter was closed. When contacted by the press for comment, Monegan first *acknowledged pressure to fire Wooten but said that he could not be certain that his own firing was connected to that issue;* he later asserted that *the dispute over Wooten was a major reason for his firing.* Palin stated on July 17 that *Monegan was not pressured to fire Wooten, nor dismissed for not doing so.*

Monegan said the subject of Wooten came up when he invited Palin to a birthday party for his cousin, state senator Lyman Hoffman, in February 2007 during the legislative session in Juneau. *"As we were walking down the stairs in the capitol building she wanted to talk to me about her former brother-in-law,"* Monegan said. *"I said, 'Ma'am, I need to keep you at arm's length with this. I can't deal about him with you." "She said, 'OK, that's a good idea.'"*

Governor Palin said there was *"absolutely no pressure ever put on Commissioner Monegan to hire or fire anybody, at any time. I did not abuse my office powers. And I don't know how to be more blunt and candid and honest, but to tell you that truth. To tell you that no pressure was ever put on anybody to fire anybody." "Never putting any pressure on him,"* added Todd Palin. But on August 13 she acknowledged that *a half dozen members of her administration had made more than two dozen calls on the matter to various state officials. "I do now have to tell Alaskans that such pressure could have been perceived to exist, although I have only now become aware of it,"* she said. Palin said, *"Many of these inquiries were completely appropriate. However, the serial nature of the contacts could be perceived as some kind of pressure, presumably at my direction."*

Chuck Kopp, who Palin had appointed to replace Monegan as public safety commissioner, *received a $10,000 state severance package after he resigned following just two weeks on the job.* Kopp, *the former Kenai chief of police,* resigned July 25 *following disclosure of a 2005 sexual harassment complaint and letter of reprimand against him.* Monegan said that he didn't get any severance package from the state.

Legislative investigation

On August 1, 2008 the *Alaska Legislature* hired an investigator, Stephen Branchflower, to review the Monegan dismissal. Legislators stated that *Palin had the legal authority to fire Monegan,* but they wanted to know *whether her action had been motivated by anger at Monegan for not firing Wooten.* The atmosphere was bipartisan *and*

Palin pledged to cooperate. Wooten remained employed as a state trooper. *She placed an aide on paid leave due to one tape-recorded phone conversation that she deemed improper,* in which the aide appeared to be acting on her behalf and complained to a trooper that Wooten had not been fired.

Several weeks *after the start of what the media referred to as "troopergate",* Palin was chosen as John McCain's running mate. On September 1, Palin asked the legislature to drop its investigation, saying that the state Personnel Board had jurisdiction over ethics issues. The Personnel Board's three members were first appointed by Palin's predecessor, and Palin reappointed one member in 2008. On September 19, the *Governor's husband and several state employees* refused to honor subpoenas, the validity of which were disputed by *Talis Colberg, Palin's appointee as Alaska's Attorney General.* On October 2, *a court rejected Colberg's challenge to the subpoenas,* and seven of the witnesses, not including Sarah and Todd Palin, eventually testified.

Branchflower Report

On October 10, 2008, the *Alaska Legislative Council* unanimously voted *to release, without endorsing,_the Branchflower Report,* in which investigator Stephen Branchflower found that *firing Monegan "was a proper and lawful exercise of her constitutional and statutory authority,"* but that Palin abused her power as governor and violated the state's Executive Branch Ethics Act *when her office pressured Monegan to fire Wooten .* The report stated that *"Governor Palin knowingly permitted a situation to continue where impermissible pressure was placed on several subordinates to advance a personal agenda, to wit: to get Trooper Michael Wooten fired."* The report also said that Palin *"permitted Todd Palin to use the Governor's office [...] to continue to contact subordinate state employees in an effort to find some way to get Trooper Wooten fired."*

On October 11, Palin's attorneys responded, *condemning the Branchflower Report as "misleading and wrong on the law"*. One of Palin's attorneys, Thomas Van Flein, said that *the Branchflower Report was an attempt to "smear the governor by innuendo."* Later that day, Governor Palin did a conference call interview with various Alaskan reporters, where she stated, *"Well, I'm very, very pleased to be cleared of any legal wrongdoing… Any hint of any kind of unethical activity there. Very pleased to be cleared of any of that."*

State Personnel Board investigation

The *State Personnel Board* (SPB) reviewed the matter *at Palin's request*. On September 15, *the Anchorage law firm of Clapp, Peterson, Van Flein, Tiemessen & Thorsness filed arguments of "no probable cause"* with the SPB *on behalf of Palin*. The SPB hired independent counsel Timothy Petumenos as an investigator. On October 24, *Palin gave three hours of depositions with the Board in St. Louis, Missouri*. On November 3, Petumenos found that *there was no probable cause to believe Palin or any other state official had violated state ethical standards.*

Resignation

A crowd estimated at 5,000 people gathered in *Fairbanks' Pioneer Park* to watch Palin turn over her office to Sean Parnell.

On July 3, 2009, Palin announced at a press conference that *she would not run for reelection in the 2010 Alaska gubernatorial election and would resign before the end of July.* Palin gave a speech offering reasons for her departure. She argued that *both she and the state have been expending an "insane" amount of time and money to address "frivolous" ethics complaints filed against her.* She also said that her decision not to seek reelection *would make her a lame duck governor.* Palin did not take questions at the press conference. A Palin aide was quoted as saying *Palin was "no longer able to do the job she had been elected to do. Essentially, the taxpayers were paying for Sarah to go to work every day and defend herself."*

2008 vice-presidential campaign

On August 24, 2008, during a general strategy meeting at the *Phoenix Ritz-Carlton* with Steve Schmidt and a few other senior advisers to the *McCain Campaign,* potential vice presidential picks were discussed. Consensus began to settle around Palin; the following day, the strategists advised McCain of their conclusions and *McCain personally called Palin who was at the Alaska State Fair.*

On August 27, she visited McCain's vacation home near *Sedona, Arizona,* where she was offered the position of vice-presidential candidate. Palin was the *only prospective running mate who had a face-to-face interview with McCain to discuss joining the ticket that week.* Nonetheless, *Palin's selection was a surprise to many as speculation had centered on other candidates,* such as *Minnesota Governor* Tim Pawlenty, *Louisiana Governor* Bobby Jindal, *former Massachusetts Governor* Mitt Romney, *United States Senator* Joe Lieberman *of Connecticut,* and *former Pennsylvania Governor* Tom Ridge.

On August 29, in Dayton, Ohio, *Republican presidential candidate John McCain* announced that *he had chosen*

Palin as his running mate. According to Jill Hazelbaker, a spokeswoman for John McCain, *he first met Palin at the National Governors Association meeting in Washington in February 2008 and came away "extraordinarily impressed."*

Palin is the *first Alaskan* and the *second woman* to run on a major U.S. party ticket. The first woman was Geraldine Ferraro, the Democratic vice-presidential nominee in 1984, who ran with former vice-president Walter Mondale. On September 3, 2008, *Palin delivered a 40-minute acceptance speech at the Republican National Convention that was well-received and watched by more than 40 million viewers.*

Several conservative commentators met Palin in the summer of 2007. Some of them, such as Bill Kristol, urged McCain to pick Palin, arguing that *her presence on the ticket* would provide a boost in enthusiasm among the religious right wing of the Republican party, while *her status as an unknown on the national scene* would also be a positive factor for McCain's campaign.

Since Palin was *largely unknown outside Alaska* before her selection by McCain, her personal life, positions, and political record *drew intense media attention and scrutiny.* On September 1, 2008, *Palin announced that her daughter Bristol was pregnant and that she would marry the father, a young man named Levi.* During this period, some Republicans felt that Palin was being subjected to unreasonable media coverage, a sentiment Palin noted in her acceptance speech. A poll taken immediately after the Republican convention found that *more than half of Americans believed that the media was "trying to hurt" Palin with negative coverage.*

During the campaign, controversy erupted over alleged differences between Palin's positions as a gubernatorial candidate and her position as a vice-presidential candidate. After McCain announced Palin as his running mate, Newsweek and Time put Palin on their magazine covers, as some of the media alleged that McCain's campaign was restricting press access to Palin by allowing only three one-on-one interviews and no press conferences with her. Palin's first major interview, *with Charles Gibson of ABC News,* met with mixed reviews. Her interview five days later with *Fox News's Sean Hannity* focused on many of the same questions from Gibson's interview. *Palin's performance in her third interview, with Katie Couric of CBS News, was widely criticized;* her poll numbers declined, Republicans expressed concern that she was becoming a political liability, and some conservative commentators called for Palin to resign from the Presidential ticket. Other conservatives remained ardent in their support for Palin, accusing the columnists of elitism. Following this interview, some Republicans, *including Mitt Romney and Bill Kristol,* questioned the McCain campaign's strategy of *sheltering Palin from unscripted encounters with the press.*

Palin was reported to have prepared intensively for the October 2 *vice-presidential debate* with Democratic vice-presidential nominee Joe Biden *at Washington University in St. Louis.* Some Republicans suggested that Palin's performance in the interviews would improve public perceptions of her debate performance by lowering expectations. Polling from CNN, Fox and CBS found that *while Palin exceeded most voters' expectations, they felt that Biden had won the debate.*

Upon returning to the campaign trail after her debate

preparation, *Palin stepped up her attacks on the Democratic candidate for President, Senator Barack Obama.* At a fundraising event, Palin explained her new aggressiveness, saying, *"There does come a time when you have to take the gloves off and that time is right now."*

Palin appeared on the television show *Saturday Night Live* on October 18. *Prior to her appearance on the show, she had been parodied several times by Tina Fey,* who was noted for her physical resemblance to the candidate. In the weeks leading up to the election, Palin had also been the subject of numerous other parodies.

The election took place on November 4, and *Obama was projected as the winner at 11:00 PM Eastern Standard Time.* In his concession speech McCain thanked Palin, calling her *"one of the best campaigners I've ever seen, and an impressive new voice in our party for reform and the principles that have always been our greatest strength."* While aides were preparing the teleprompter for McCain's speech, *they found a concession speech written for Palin by Bush speechwriter Matthew Scully.* Two members of McCain's staff, Steve Schmidt and Mark Salter, told Palin that *there was no tradition of Election Night speeches by running mates,* and that she would not be speaking. *Palin appealed to McCain, who agreed with his staff.*

After the 2008 election

Palin was selected as one of America's *"Top 10 Most Fascinating People"* of 2008 for a Barbara Walters ABC special on December 4, 2008. She was the first guest on *commentator Glenn Beck's Fox News television show* on January 19, 2009, commenting on President Barack Obama that he was her president and that she would assist in any way to bring progress to the nation without abandoning her conservative views.

On January 27, 2009, Palin formed the *political action committee, SarahPAC*. The organization which describes itself as *an advocate of "energy independence,"* supports candidates for federal and state office. Following her resignation as Governor, Palin announced her intention *to campaign "on behalf of candidates who believe in the right things, regardless of their party label or affiliation."* It was reported that SarahPAC had raised nearly $1,000,000 by July 13, 2009, and that *only 28 of the 709 donations over $200 had come from Alaska residents*. A legal defense fund has also been set up to help Gov. Palin challenge ethics complaints, and it had collected approximately $250,000 as of mid July 2009.

Going Rogue

In November 2009, Palin released *Going Rogue: An American Life*, which quickly became a bestseller. Palin made a number of media appearances to promote the book, including a widely publicized interview on November 16, 2009 with Oprah Winfrey.

Going Rogue: An American Life is the *New York Times #1 best seller by former American Vice Presidential candidate Sarah Palin,* co-written by Lynn Vincent of San Diego, and edited by Adam Bellow for HarperCollins. The *memoir* was released on November 17, 2009, and became *the third political memoir in history to sell more than 1 million copies.* The book's title is a reference to a phrase that arose during the latter part of the *2008 presidential campaign*. Palin embraced it after the question, *"Has Sarah Palin 'gone rogue'?",* appeared in the lead of an article in the magazine, *Slate*. The subtitle, *"An American Life",* is the same as that of Ronald Reagan's 1990 autobiography.

2012 speculation

Palin's high profile in the 2008 presidential campaign fueled speculation that *she may run for the Republican presidential nomination in 2012,* and as of November 2008, there is an active *"Draft Palin" movement.* In December 2008, she campaigned for Sen. Saxby Chambliss of Georgia in his bid to be re-elected to the Senate in the run-off election. Chambliss went on to win by a larger than expected margin, and he credited Palin with *drumming up support from the conservative base of the Republican Party.* This fueled mounting speculation that Palin may run for president herself in 2012.

On the question of seeking the Presidency, Palin told CNN that, *"right now I cannot even imagine running for national office in 2012."* She has, *however,* left the door open for a future presidential run, whether it be in 2012 or at a later date.

A few polls were taken after the 2008 election on the subject of Palin's future as a presidential candidate. At the *Conservative Political Action Conference* in February 2009, a straw poll was held to determine who conservatives would be most likely to support for president in 2012. *Palin came in third, with 13%, tying Texas Congressman Ron Paul.* Former Massachusetts Governor Mitt Romney came in first with 20%, followed by Louisiana Governor Bobby Jindal with 14%. A June 2009 *CNN/Opinion Research Corporation* national poll *showed Palin as the 2012 presidential co-favorite of the Republican electorate along with Romney and Mike Huckabee.* The same month, a *Pew Research Center poll* found that *equal amounts of the general public viewed Palin favorably versus unfavorably,* with few having no opinion. This was roughly consistent with her ratings during the vice-presidential campaign. Among Republicans, however, her favorability ratings were very high, and greater than those for several other Republican political figures.

Family and religion

Palin describes herself as a *hockey mom.* The Palins have five children: sons Track (b. 1989) and Trig Paxson Van (b. 2008), and daughters Bristol Sheeran Marie (b. 1990), Willow (b. 1995), and Piper (b. 2001). Track enlisted in the U.S. Army on September 11, 2007, and was subsequently assigned to an infantry brigade. He and his unit deployed to Iraq in September 2008 for 12 months. Palin's youngest child, Trig, was prenatally diagnosed with Down syndrome. Palin has one grandchild, a boy named Tripp Easton Mitchell Johnston, who was born to her eldest daughter Bristol, in 2008. Sarah's husband Todd works for the British oil company BP as an oil-field production operator and owns a commercial fishing business.

Palin was born into a Roman Catholic family. Later, her family joined the *Wasilla Assembly of God, a Pentecostal church,* which she attended until 2002. Palin then switched to the *Wasilla Bible Church* because, she said, *she preferred the children's ministries offered there.* When in Juneau, she attends the *Juneau Christian Center.* Palin described herself in an interview as a *"Bible-believing Christian."* After the *Republican National Convention,* a spokesperson for the McCain campaign told CNN that *Palin "doesn't consider herself Pentecostal"* and *has "deep religious convictions."*

In keeping with her religious background, *Palin talked in a PBS interview of how her favorite writer is C. S. Lewis.*

Political positions

Palin has been a registered Republican since 1982, and has described the Republican Party platform as *"the right agenda for America."*

Palin is a *social conservative.*

Palin opposes *same-sex marriage.*

Palin opposes *embryonic stem cell research,* and abortion, calling herself "as *pro-life* as any candidate can be." She has referred to *abortion* as an "atrocity," but opposes sanctions against women who obtain an abortion. She supports laws requiring *parental consent* for minors seeking an abortion.

Palin supports allowing the discussion of *creationism* in public schools, but is not in favor of teaching it as part of the curriculum. She supports sex education in public schools that *encourages abstinence* but also *discusses birth control.*

A lifetime member of the *National Rifle Association* (NRA), Palin believes the *right to bear arms* includes handgun possession, is *against a ban on semi-automatic assault weapons,* and supports *gun safety education for youth.*

Palin supports *capital punishment for adults who murder children and other innocent people.*

Palin has promoted oil and natural gas resource exploration in Alaska, including in the *Arctic National Wildlife Refuge* (ANWR).

Palin has expressed skepticism about the *causes of global warming,* but agrees that "man's activities certainly can be contributing to the issue" *and that action should be taken.*

Palin is opposed to *cap-and-trade proposals* such as

the *American Clean Energy and Security Act.*

On *foreign policy,* Palin supported the Bush Administration's policies in Iraq, but is concerned that *"dependence on foreign energy"* may be obstructing efforts to *"have an exit plan in place."*

Palin supports *preemptive military action* in the face of an imminent threat, and supports U.S. military operations in Pakistan.

Palin supports *NATO membership for Ukraine and Georgia,* and affirms that if Russia invaded a NATO member, the United States *should meet its treaty obligations.*

Palin has been an outspoken opponent of *Congress' plans for health care reform,* claiming it would include *what she called "death panels,"* which would threaten handicapped people such as her son Trig.

Palin opposed *end-of-life advance directives* mentioned in page 425 of a health care bill.

Palin *declared April 16 2008 Healthcare Decisions Day* in part so that *"more citizens will execute advance directives."*

Public image

During the campaign, *Palin evoked a more strongly divided response than Joe Biden* among voters. A plurality of the television audience rated Biden's performance higher at *the 2008 vice-presidential debate.*

Media outlets repeated Palin's statement that *she "stood up to Big Oil"* when she resigned *after 11 months as the head of the Alaska Oil and Gas Conservation Commission, due to abuses she witnessed involving other Republican commissioners and their ties to energy companies and energy lobbyists,* and again when she *raised taxes on oil companies as governor.*

Others have said that Palin is *a "friend of Big Oil"* due to her advocacy of oil exploration and development including drilling in the *Arctic National Wildlife Refuge* (ANWR) and the *de-listing of the polar bear as an endangered species.* The *National Organization for Women,* which endorsed Obama, made clear that *it would not support Palin,* and made its support for her opponent publicly known. The *National Rifle Association* said nothing specific about *Palin's position on gun legislation,* but concluded that *she would be "one of the most pro-gun vice-presidents in American history."*

Following the presidential election, 69% of Republicans felt Palin had helped John McCain's bid, while 20% felt Palin hurt. In the same poll, 71% of Republicans stated Palin had been the right choice. An article by *Robert Jones & Daniel Cox, "Beyond the Spin",* in *Religion Dispatches,* uses *a "post-election" surve*y to show that *McCain's choice of Palin split likely Republican voters.* She scored *highly* with White evangelicals but lost support for McCain *among White Roman Catholics.*

2
Gov. Palin on Environment

Opposed protections for salmon from mining contamination

This month, Ms. Palin issued a last-minute statement of opposition to a ballot measure that would have provided added protections for salmon from potential contamination from mining, an action seen as crucial to its defeat.

Source: New York Times, pp. A1 & A10, "An Outsider Who Charms" Aug 29, 2008

Sue US government to stop listing polar bear as endangered

Governor Sarah Palin announced today the State of Alaska has filed a lawsuit in U.S. District Court for the District of Columbia seeking to overturn Interior Secretary Dirk Kempthorne's decision to list the polar bear as threatened under the Endangered Species Act.

This action follows written notice given more than 60 days ago, asking that the regulation listing the polar bear as threatened be withdrawn. "We believe that the Service's decision to list the polar bear was not based on the best scientific and commercial data available," Governor Palin said.

The Service's analysis failed to adequately consider the polar bears' survival through prior warming periods, and its findings that the polar bear is threatened by sea-ice habitat loss are not warranted. The Service also failed to adequately consider the existing regulatory mechanisms which have resulted in a sustainable worldwide polar bear population that has more than doubled in number over the last 40 years to 20,000-25,000 bears.

Source: *Alaska Governor's Office: press release, "Polar Bear"* Aug 4, 2008

We must encourage timber, mining, drilling, & fishing

Industry knows we want responsible development. Anadarko will drill Alaska's first-ever gas-targeted wells on the North Slope. Chevron, FEX, Renaissance—many others are exploring. That's ratification of AGIA's promise to make investments profitable for industrious explorers. There's more we can do to ramp up development. Our new reservoir study can increase development and we will ensure better, publicly supported project coordination. To cultivate timber and agriculture, we're encouraging responsible, economic efforts to revitalize our once-robust industries. We can and must continue to develop our economy, because we cannot and must not rely so heavily on federal government earmarks.

Source: *2008 State of the State Address to 25th Alaska Legislature* Jan 15, 2008

Wolf predator control is important for subsistence hunters

Gov. Palin criticized Congressman George Miller's (D-CA) legislation to eliminate an important element of wildlife management by the State of Alaska. "Moose & caribou are important food for Alaskans, & Rep. Miller's bill threatens that food supply," said Gov. Palin. "Rep. Miller doesn't understand rural Alaska, doesn't comprehend wildlife management in the North, and doesn't appreciate the Tenth Amendment that gives states the right to manage their own affairs."

Miller's bill would ban the shooting of wolves from aircraft, a component of moose and caribou management plans in five specific areas of Alaska. Contrary to what Rep. Miller said in Washington yesterday, there is no "aerial hunting" of wolves in Alaska, Palin said. "Our science-driven and abundance-based predator management program involves volunteers who are permitted to use aircraft to kill some predators where we are trying to increase opportunities for Alaskans to put healthy food on their families' dinner tables. It is not hunting."

*Source: **Alaska Governor's Office: Press release 07-197, "Wildlife"** Sep 26, 2007*

Feds shouldn't list beluga whales as endangered

Gov. Palin has told the federal government that the state is extremely concerned about a proposal to list Cook Inlet beluga whales as an endangered species, and urged the National Marine Fisheries Service (NMFS) not to list the species.

"Our scientist feel confident that it would be unwarranted to list Cook Inlet belugas now," Gov. Palin said. "Seven years ago, NMFS determined that these whales weren't endangered, and since then, we've actually seen the beginnings of an increase in their population. We are all doing everything we can to help protect these important marine mammals."

The state submitted 95 pages of data and formal comments to NMFS on the proposed listing, pointing out that the Cook Inlet stock of belugas is recovering from an "unsustainable harvest" in the early 1990s. "I am especially concerned that an unnecessary federal listing and designation of critical habitat would do serious long-term damage to the vibrant economy of the Cook Inlet area," Palin said.

Source: **Alaska Governor's Office: Press release 07-175, "Beluga"** Aug 7, 2007

Provide stability in regulations for developers

I'm keenly aware of sharply declining production from North Slope fields. The amount of oil currently flowing through the Pipeline is less than half of what it was at its peak. We must look to responsible development throughout the state—from the Slope all the way down to Southeast—every region participating! From further oil and gas development, to fishing, mining, timber, and tourism, these developments remain the core of our state. We provide stability in regulations for our developers.

Source: *2007 State of the State Address to 24th Alaska Legislature Jan 17, 2007*

Convince the rest of the nation to open ANWR

The standard should be no different for industry. Ironically, we're trying to convince the rest of the nation to open ANWR, but we can't even get our own Pt. Thomson, which is right on the edge of ANWR, developed! We are ready for that gas to be tapped so we can fill a natural gas pipeline. I promise to vigorously defend Alaska's rights, as resource owners, to develop and receive appropriate value for our resources.

Source: 2007 State of the State Address to 24th Alaska Legislature Jan 17, 2007

Fish platform: "Resource First" philosophy
COMMERCIAL FISHING: Fish Platform: Do What's Right For Alaska's Fishing Communities
- "Resource First" Philosophy
- Professional ADF&G Management with Adequate Funding
- Fishery Advisor
- Balanced Board and Council Appointments
- Aggressive Marketing Campaign
- No Fish Farming allowed

I am not only a champion for Alaska's fishing industry, but I am a part of it. My family is proud to be a Bristol Bay fishing family. If we manage for abundance, we should have enough fish for all our needs.

Source: Palin-Parnell campaign booklet: New Energy for Alaska Nov 3, 2006

Rail provides critical link for business development
- The railroad provides a critical link to Interior Alaska for hauling equipment & materials, as well as passengers.
- Rail service & use has improved greatly over the past few years. The system is being managed, maintained, and upgraded to better standards.
- Rail development is ideal for transport of heavy items. If it is economically beneficial over the long term, rail should be utilized open up those areas of Alaska currently not served by roads in order to support business development.

Source: Palin-Parnell campaign booklet: New Energy for Alaska Nov 3, 2006

Supports "Roads to Resources": subsidized access to mines

When it comes to spending state money, Palin is generally conservative. Yet Palin supports the state's *"roads to resources program,"* which funds roads to mines and other natural resources projects such as oil and gas.

Source: Anchorage Daily News: 2006 gubernatorial candidate profile Oct 31, 2006

Don't duplicate effort in monitoring cruise ship emissions

Palin questioned environmental aspects of the new cruise ship law in an Oct. 17 letter to the Alaska Travel Industry Association, the state's major tourism group. Palin questioned whether the new environmental monitoring is "redundant" under state law and she said no other Alaska business faces the consumer disclosures now required for cruise lines. Palin worried about the law's environmental enforcement and its requirement for cruise lines to disclose their commissions for channeling passengers to flightseeing companies, rafting businesses, gift shops and other on-shore vendors.

The state Departments of Environmental Conservation and state Department of Revenue are now writing the regulations to enforce the taxes, environmental permits and disclosure rules. The new taxes and rules go into effect Dec. 17.

Source: Anchorage Daily News: 2006 gubernatorial candidate profile Oct 30, 2006

Don't amend AK constitution for rural subsistence

3
Sarah Palin Memoirs
Highlights of 'Going Rogue'

This chapter is a compilation of Sarah Palin's statements extracted from her book, *"Going Rogue: An American Life."*

— — —

By the time I was thirty-eight, my second term [as mayor] was winding down and I was about to be term-limited out of office. Meanwhile, several people approached me saying they hoped I'd stay in public service. Not politicos, just ordinary people.

As president of the Conference of Mayors, I saw so many needs around the state, places where I felt I could help. But I had no interest in running for the state legislature. I did not think I would do well in a place where you had to scratch disagreeable backs in order to secure a nameplate in the caucus.

— — —

Having advocated for local control across the state as president of the Alaska Conference of Mayors, I added that principle to my campaign platform. I had great respect for the need for state government to preserve locally enacted policies. Likewise, I believed that national leaders have a responsibility to respect the Tenth Amendment and keep their hands off the states. It's the old Jeffersonian view that the affairs of the citizens are best left in their own hands.

— — —

I guess Murkowski took me seriously when I said my most important issues were energy and resource development. A couple of months into his administration, he offered me a job as chairman of the **Alaska Oil and Gas Conservation Commission** (**AOGCC**). It was confirmation that having lost out on the lieutenant governor's position and the U.S. Senate appointment were actually blessings.

More than 85% of the state's budget is built on petroleum-based energy revenues. For more than thirty years the big oil companies like British Petroleum (BP), ExxonMobile, and ConocoPhillips have extracted the oil underneath Alaska lands and sold billions of barrels of it to very hungry markets. But oil is not a renewable resource. Once it's gone, it's gone, so it has to be dealt with prudently. [ed., oil might be self renewable, *see page 78.*]

Many Alaskans were aware that these huge multinational energy corporations had been leasing oil-rich chunks of land on the North Slope, but were just sitting on the leases, in some cases for decades. And as long as they held the leases, other companies couldn't come in and compete for the right to tap our resources, so parts of the oil basis were essentially locked up.

— — —

I finally decided to toss my hat in the ring to replace Frank Murkowski as governor, and I was having a ball working long, intense days. By the end of that summer, the bottom line for me was clear: voters wanted change, and they should have a straightforward choice about what kind of change it would be. As always, Todd supported me and encouraged me to do it. So on Alaska Day, October 18, 2005, I kicked off the gubernatorial campaign with about fifty friends, family, and reporters in my living room. It was also Bristol's fifteenth birthday, so of course, we had cake.

— — —

Our campaign would focus on cleaning house in government and facilitating the private-sector development of energy resources, specifically ramping up production of America's energy supplies and building the 3,000-mile, $40 billion natural gas pipeline that other administrations had been promising to build for decades. It would ultimately go from the North Slope to hungry Midwest markets out of a Chicago hub. I was determined that Alaska was going to start contributing more to the nation.

— — —

I would gather the information I needed and base my decisions on principle and sound ideas, not cronyism or political expediency. I ran on my record as an executive and told Alaska voters that I would govern according to conservative principles, and if I were to err, would be on the side of those principles. Like stars in the northern sky, Alaska has hundreds of tiny town and villages flung across it, and the people who live in them are the state's heart and soul. When we visited, sometimes whole towns turned out, from little kids to Native elders bearing **akutaq** [*eskimo ice cream*] and blueberry muffins and salmon strips.

— — —

Triumph on November 7, 2006!

On election night, hundreds of us filed into a ballroom at the Hotel Captain Cook to celebrate our victory. We were so thrilled and thankful — and finally tired — as the results poured in. We won with nearly half the vote in a six-way race.

— — —

All through Alaska's history, the inaugural swearing in had taken place in the capital city of Juneau. But in a break with tradition, I selected Fairbanks, the Golden Heart City, as the location for the December 4, ceremony. The fiftieth anniversary of statehood would take place during our term, so we wanted to celebrate the Alaska Constitution, which was written in Fairbanks. That was what I wanted to honor that day. Thanks to our state's simple and concise founding documents, our founding mothers and fathers had provided a level of opportunity and prosperity that other states, even other countries, could only dream of. I believed then — and still do now — that in addition to God's grace, the credit for Alaska's prosperity should be given to our Constitution's framers.

— — —

To kick off the Palin-Parnell agenda, we started with the natural gas pipeline on our first day in office.

For Alaskans, the term "gasline" is as familiar as "irrigation" is to Californians or "Wall Street" is to New Yorkers. Except that Californians and New Yorkers already reap the benefits of these economic lifelines, while Alaskans have been waiting more than fifty years to realize the benefits of the state's vast reserves of natural gas. At least 35 trillion cubic feet of proven natural gas reserves lie untapped on the North Slope, and geologists say there are hundreds of trillions more, both on- *and* offshore.

Construction of a gas pipeline to transport this safe, clean energy supply to the Lower 48 was originally authorized by the **Federal Energy Regulatory Commission (FERC)** in 1979. At the time, a lot of folks had high hopes. Not only would the pipeline become a second economic pillar of the state creating jobs and development opportunities, but it would reduce our dependence on foreign supplies and therefore our reliance on unfriendly nations,

Cheap natural gas from other countries had delayed the project for years. And for years the big producers who held leases on the gas fields sat on their contracts, preferring instead to develop projects in countries with fewer labor and environmental restrictions. It was unfortunate that our government's well-meaning policies had driven producers to other parts of the world where there were no restraints on their activities. That was no way to protect the environment or heal the economy.

With my background, I understood the concerns of all the parties: as a free-market capitalist I understood the bottom line for the oil producers; as the spouse of an oil worker I understood the Slopers and their families' reliance on oil jobs; as a mayor I understood the communities' dependence on oil's economic contributions; as a lover of the land I understood as well the environmentalists' and Alaska Natives' concerns.

Any corporate CEO is tasked with looking out for the

bottom line. Our state Constitution stipulates that **the citizens actually own our natural resources.** Oil companies would partner with Alaskans to develop our resources, and the corporations would make decisions based on the best interests of their shareholders, and that was fine. But in fulfillment of my oath, I would make decisions based on the best interests of *our* shareholders, the people of Alaska.

So in my Anchorage office, we established the ground rules for the gasline team. Our goal was to commercialize Alaska's treasure of oil and gas by opening up the North Slope basin to long-term exploration and production, thus creating jobs and ensuring a stable energy supply.

— — —

Under Murkowski's administration, gasline renegotiation had taken place behind closed doors.

My friend Tom had told Murkowski one too many times that the secret gasline deal he was negotiating with ExxonMobile, BP, and ConocoPhillips violated the state's Constitution. Among other things, his approach reliquished state sovereignty, and would unwisely lock in tax rates for decades into the future despite volatility in the markets.

So I put my name and commitment behind a proposal to open bidding to the private sector.

Our approach to moving the gasline forward was both innovative and simple: Explain the importance of gasline development to ordinary Alaskans. And get them involved. That meant our war room became every kitchen table, town hall, classroom, and living room across the Last Frontier.

We reached out. We asked citizens. "These are your

resources, so what do *you* think?"

Internally, our natural gas mantra was *"Greenies, Grannies, and Gunnies."*

Greenies: natural gas is the cleanest nonrenewable fuel.

Grannies: production of a domestic supply from Alaska would help those on fixed incomes, such as the elderly, by increasing supply and lowering costs in a more stable price environment.

Gunnies: Alaska's energy supplies would help lead America toward energy independence and greater national security.

Greenies, Grannies, and Gunnies. So Alaskan. So politically incorrect. Perfect.

— — —

The size of Alaska is difficult to comprehend for anyone living in the Lower 48. It is huge, one-fifth the size of the entire continental U.S. When the kids and I moved to Juneau in January 2007, Todd and I worked more than 1,300 miles apart. Adding to the challenge, you can't drive between Prudhoe Bay and our capital city, of course, even if you were up for a four-day road trip. In fact no one can drive to Juneau. You can fly in or hop a ferry, but not many people want to brave the frigid swells on the Inside passage waterways in January during the legislative session, so Juneau's always been known as the most inaccessible state capital in America. I wanted to change that too.

About a two-hour flight from Anchorage, Juneau sits at the base of Mount Juneau, enclosed by Auke Bay and hemmed in by dense forests. I think it's the nation's prettiest capital.

I also trimmed the state's food budget by keeping our home's freezer stocked with the world seafood we caught ourselves, as well as organic protein sources hunted by friends and family. We kept an interesting variety of food that way. If any vegans came over for dinner, I could whip them up a salad, then explain my philosophy on being a carnivore: *If God had not intended for us to eat animals, how come He made them out of meat?*

As Governor, though, hunting *was* an issue. I would face pressure from Hollywood to halt hunting, ban guns, and end our state's wildlife management practices, such as controlling predators. I said no to all of that nonsense: gun bans would destroy the Second Amendment, and as a life-long member of the NRA (Alaska has the highest NRA membership per capita in the nation), I had plenty of backup when telling Hollywood liberals what I thought of their asinine plans to ban guns. And we had to control predators, such as wolves, that were decimating the moose and caribou herds that feed our communities. People outside of Alaska are often clueless about our reliance on natural food sources. But as the ninety-year old Alaska Native leader Sydney Hunnington told Todd, "Nowadays, common sense is an endangered species."

Managing a $14 billion budget as the chief executive of the largest state in the Union with thousands of employees is more complex than managing a city like Wasilla, and certainly weightier than managing a household of seven.

But lessons learned on the micro level still apply to the macro. Just as my family couldn't fund every item on our wish list, and had to live within our means as well as save for the future, I felt we needed to do that for the state. I had four core principles as the foundation of our budget: live within our means, expand resource development and industry, focus on core services (education, infrastructure, and public safety), and save for the future. And I reminded my staff: never forget you're spending other people's money, that should make us more prudent and serious than anything.

Almost all of our state budget depends on development of Alaska's energy resources. The petroleum resource is non renewable. When it's gone, it's gone. Not only is it finite, its value fluctuates. In 1999, the price of a barrel of oil was $9; in 2008, it was $140. Price is dependent upon many factors — a war in a third world country, a hurricane off the coast, an angry petro-dictator, new oil discoveries in foreign lands. And our revenue department has to estimate every year what the price of a barrel of oil will be in order for us to build the budget.

Alaskan's know the pain of wildly fluctuating oil prices. We learned our lesson about saving for the future the hard way. During the heyday of the Trans-Alaska Pipeline, we were living the good life. The price of oil was high and the boom was on, creating a gold rush of state revenue, which government spent as quickly as possible. We were still a vast, undeveloped frontier outpost in need of infrastructure. So the state spent fast.

Then the smack-down: oil bottomed out at $9 a barrel. When the next boom came during my administration, we were determined to be conservative and accountable to future generations. (As Thomas Paine said in 1776: "If there must be trouble, let it be in my day, that my children may have peace.")

And so began our marathon budget breakdown. It was late June 2007, just after the solstice, and we worked late into the night with the warm midnight sun still pouring through my office windows.

— — —

My philosophy has always been that the most responsive and responsible level of government is the local level. Local government is best able to prioritize services and projects. That's the basis of the Tenth Amendment to the U.S. Constitution, which paraphrased, says that the powers not delegated specifically to the federal government or prohibited by the states are reserved to the states or the people themselves.

— — —

Ordinary Alaskans were expressing outrage at what was going on in Juneau, and I had promised to clean house. Remember the young political appointee who was supposed to be the ethics supervisor over IOGCC? In 2006, he was working as Governor Murkowski's chief legislative aide, representing the state in gasoline negotiations with ExxonMobile and other companies. A few months later, he was earning $10,000 a month lobbying the state for ExxonMobile. The public's obvious question: whose side are these guys on?

We were determined to keep the pressure on. That pressure paid off when legislators approved an omnibus ethics bill that imposed criminal penalties on lawmakers who traded votes for campaign contributions. Any legislator convicted of a felony would forfeit his state pension.

— — —

As with ethics reform, my team and I were determined to fundamentally change the game when it came to the natural gas pipeline. Instead of negotiating behind closed doors with the monopolistic industry, we wanted to get back to competitive free-market principles, ethically employed.

This was a multibillion-dollar project, the largest private-sector energy project in North American history. It was a once-in-a-lifetime opportunity. So we had to demand that the resource owners' needs be met. To get the project off the ground after decades of politicians just talking about it, we tried a "newfangled" approach: free market principles. We asked willing and able companies to compete for the right to build Alaska's gasline. Our approach would be open and transparent, with no behind-closed-door deals.

The project would cost the private sector a tremendous amount in government fees and prep work to get through local, state, and federal regulatory and environmental processes, so it made sense, along with the state's number of must-haves, for us to put some skin in the game by reimbursing the winning bidder for some of the up-front bureaucratic costs.

Therefore, in crafting what would become the landmark **Alaska Gasline Inducement Act**, or **AGIA**, we promised to reimburse up to $500 million in matching funds for the exclusive gasline license.

Still, Big Oil slammed us in the media — again, confirmation that we were making the right decisions. Soon after, we introduced AGIA to the legislature. That new word, "ah-gee-ah," quickly became part of the 49th State's vernacular. After much debate, the legislature adopted AGIA. In the end, only *one* lawmaker voted against the measure.

— — —

I discussed with representatives of other oil- and gas-producing states what America's needs are and how we can become energy-independent. I also assumed chairmanship of the **Interstate Oil and Gas Compact Commission (IOGCC)**, where I could help influence congress and the White House on energy and security issues.

— — —

"Go to hell, but resign first."
This particular crisp instruction was sent to DNR Commissioner Tom Irwin by a North Slope oil services company employee. [**(DNR) Department of Natural Resources**]
Irwin's recent actions had prompted the e-mail.
For the twenty-second time, ExxonMobile had submitted its plan to begin drilling in the Point Thomson Unit but still had not drilled. These domestic supplies of energy were needed. So with my full support, Tom had played hardball and took steps to prove that ExxonMobile was in default of its lease agreements.
My administration announced that for the state's and country's sake, ExxonMobile would no longer be allowed to just warehouse America's resources. After all these decades, if the largest company in the world wasn't going to

abide by its contracts to drill, we would rebid the leases and find a company that would.

That resulted in the kind note to Tom from an industry player about this employment future and eternal destination.

— — —

Adjacent to the much-discussed ANWR area, Point Thomson is a North Slope parcel of state-owned land that holds trillions of cubic feet of clean natural gas and an equally enormous amount of oil. The leases in question were the subject of a prior expansion agreement that would substantially enlarge the area in which ExxonMobile was permitted to drill. Of course, the big question was, why would DNR approve an expansion when ExxonMobile had sat on the unit for more than twenty-five years and had never successfully enlarged the area in which ExxonMobile had sat on the unit for more than twenty-five years and had never successfully sunk a drill bit?

— — —

When you deal with oil executives, you have to remember that they are used to winning. They also spend a lot of time in foreign countries dealing with leaders who carry pistols and whose bodyguards carry AK-47s. Meanwhile, the executives themselves are armed with bottomless bank accounts and highly trained platoons of fire-breathing lawyers. Thus reminding our friends in Big Oil that they have a contract that they're obligated to fulfill was really not going to scare them. A $20 million fine is "Pocket" change. But with their leases on the line — permanently — the question

ExxonMobile executives finally had to ask themselves was, do we really want to give up prime parcels that are loaded with billions of dollars' worth of natural resources that the public and our shareholders want us to develop? As AOGCC chair, when I wasn't butting heads with the state GOP, I was getting a thorough education in issues surrounding oil and gas recovery and production.

— — —

Two days after my first State of the State Address, I spoke to a group of energy explorers at an industry breakfast. It provided me with the perfect opportunity to set that stage and let our most powerful industry know how I would lead. Among the messages that I wished to send: Alaska is now open for business.

"You in the industry make your living by providing the goods and services necessary to get Alaska's resources to market," I said. "You live by contracts and legal obligations . . . Leases and unit agreements are contracts. Lessees must develop the public's resources or give back their leases."

ExxonMobile needed to develop now or let others compete to do so. In the larger scheme of things, I also knew that unless we accessed our known reserves on state lands, it would be more difficult to argue for access to federal lands such a ANWR. We had to prove we could do so safely and ethically before the Feds would let us develop in more controversial areas. As a state chief executive sitting across the table from well-heeled, lawyered-up executives, it was a given: you have to be committed to the position that is right for the people who hired you. You can't blink.

And we didn't.

Once we put our foot down, we won ruling after ruling after ruling. ... When you know you've made the right call, you stand your ground. DNR had made the right call. We would now see development.

Victory!

Two years into our term, Rolligons packed with drilling equipment started driving up the long ice road to Point Thomson to deploy hundreds of new workers in their hard hats and steel-toed boots. Exxon began ordering parts and supplies and buying equipment in order to develop rich resources for the industry, the state, and the nation. This was a bipartisan victory that created the mutually beneficial relationship between government and industry we had sought all along.

— — —

In the months following the AGIA vote, I was glad I'd trained for marathons. I'm superstitious about cutting any corners when I jog, believing the few extra steps can make a difference in the long race.

The competitive bidding process we created with AGIA unlocked the Big Three oil companies' development monopoly and threw open Alaska's doors to true competition and free enterprise. Suddenly, even other nations were bidding on the multibillion dollar project.

Early in 2008, the DNR and revenue commissioners finally announced their AGIA recommendation: the Calgary-based pipeline building giant TransCanada-Alaska, a firm that had not only met every single enforceable requirement of AGIA but exceeded them. We were ecstatic. *I* was ecstatic: there would be hundreds of steps yet to take, but we could almost envision the tape draped across the finish line.

— — —

On Friday, August 1, 2008, Alaskans won again: the legislature overwhelmingly voted to award the AGIA license to TransCanada-Alaska. We still had a long way to go until our clean, safe energy flowed south to the Lower 48, but after a thirty-year wait, we had turned the idea of commercializing our natural gas for Alaska's economic future from pipe *dream* to pipe*line*.

I had been elected governor of the state I loved. And in just the past year, we had kicked off the pipeline, overhauled ethics in state government, slashed state spending with my vetoes, saved for the future, and put money back into the hands of the people. Plus, we radically changed the way Alaskans would be secured in the futures with the natural resources they owned.

— — —

"Our Constitution demands that Alaskans come first. It will keep my compass pointed true north. It's the tool to build Alaska with strength and with order." I hit on the issues critical to our state: responsible energy resource development, cleaning up corruption, putting Alaskans to work in good jobs, reforming education, and nurturing that most precious resource — our children.

I emphasized my priorities of improving public safety and tackling substance abuse. Then I concluded with plain talk on the role of government, stressing fiscal restraint and the importance of competition and free enterprise. "Alaskans, hold me accountable, and right back at you!" I said.

"I'll expect a lot from you, too! Take responsibility for your family and for your futures. Don't think you need government to take care of all needs and to make your decisions for you. More government isn't the answer because you have ability, because you are Alaskans, and you live in a land that God, with incredible benevolence, decided to overwhelmingly bless."

We *were* shaking things up — and there'd be new energy for a new future.

— — —

My mission in office: to develop our state's resources in the best interests of the environment and of the people — including getting a gasline built. Ronald Reagan's principles: pick your departments and staff to implement your vision in other areas. Reagan concentrated on a few key issues and knocked them out of the park. That gave him the political capital to effect change in many other policy areas. I knew if I kept my campaign promise of overhauling the state in the areas of resource development, fiscal restraint, and ethical government, I would also be able to turn attention to equally urgent issues such as education, services for special needs and the elderly, job training, unemployment, and social ills in rural Alaska. We'd be able to do so with reprioritized funding to help the private sector provide opportunities in a way that would help Alaskans stand tall and independent.

— — —

We don't trust utopian promises from politicians. The role of government is not to perfect us but to protect us — to protect our inalienable rights. The role of government in a civil society is to protect the individual and to establish a social contract so the we can live together in peace.

— — —

Our prosperity has been driven by steady, abundant, affordable energy supplies. In Alaska, we understand the inherent link between energy and prosperity, energy and opportunity, and energy and security. I believe Alaska will lead the nation in developing both renewable and non renewable resources. I've always advocated an "all of the above" approach to energy production, and I support the harnessing of alternative sources of energy such as wind, solar, and geothermal. **Using renewable sources means developing nuclear energy, too.**

— — —

Some people ask whether we are still a republic, or whether we are becoming an empire, doomed to fade away like all the other empires once thought to be invincible.

We are still a republic. We are certainly not doomed to fade away. And we have no desire to be an empire. We don't want to colonize other countries or force our ideals on them. But we have been given a unique responsibility: to show the world the meaning and the rewards of freedom. America, as Reagan said, is "the abiding alternative to tyranny." We must remain the shining City on a Hill to all who seek freedom and prosperity.

— — —

But we must reawaken our belief in the principles that underlie our Constitution and the power we have when individuals stand together.

When we empower ourselves to stand up together, we become an even more blessed and prosperous nation. And we become a more generous nation, too — a nation that has proved for more than two centuries its willingness to share its blessings with others.`

"I don't believe that God put us on earth to be ordinary"
— *Going Rogue, page 1*

"There's no better training ground for politics than motherhood." — Going Rogue, p.115

"The Role of government is not to perfect us but to protect us — to protect our in alienable rights."
— *Going Rogue, p.386*

*"Gun bans will destroy the Second Amendment.
We have to destroy predators."*
— *Going Rogue, p.133*

"National leaders have a responsibility to respect the Tenth Amendment and keep their hands off the states. It's the old Jeffersonian view that the affairs of the citizens are best left in their own hands." — *Going Rogue, p.85*

". . . the citizens actually own our natural resources."
  — *Going Rogue, p.126*

"'For I know the plans that I have for you,' declares the Lord. 'Plans for peace and not for calamity, to give you a future and a hope. When you call upon Me I will hear you, when you search for me you will find Me; if you seek Me with all your heart.'"
— *Jeremiah 29:11-13, Going Rogue, p.103*

NEW KID ON THE BLOCK

Gov. Elect Debra Medina

4
Gov. Elect Debra Medina
Viable Candidate For Texas Governor

Scott Brown's shocking victory is a mixed blessing for the cause of freedom. On one hand it has put a major roadblock in the path towards Obama Care. On the other hand Scott Brown is a big government Republican. So far there are no signs that true reform is taking place in the GOP.

The people in control of the party during the worst two consecutive election cycle defeats in GOP history are still in control of the leadership nationally. This is why a Debra Medina victory is a tremendous opportunity to return to the original constitutionally limited government given us by the founders.

Why is it that important for Medina to win? Because Texas is that important. Texas is the flagship state of the Republican Party. The Texas GOP is the biggest "Grand Old Party" (Republican) in the Nation. It's also, heavily controlled by the Bush/McCain wing.

The two establishment candidates, Governor Rick Perry and Senator Kay Bailey Hutchison represent two of the worst examples of compromised career politicians. Both Perry's & Hutchinson's record are typical of out of touch elitists. Like Obama, Perry repeatedly tried to cram the Trans Texas Corridor, and the tolling of existing roads, down the throats of Texans who clearly are against it by huge margins in poll after poll. Senator Hutchinson exhibited the same Obama like behavior in voting for TARP, against the overwhelming opposition of her constituents, to TARP.

Only the uninformed would expect either Perry or Hutchinson to be any different than they have been their entire political careers. This country will not survive with two socialist political parties. Like it or not, most Republicans are really FDR Democrats.

Virtually all the New Deal is vigorously supported by and even expanded by Republicans. The GOP of today is not the same "Grand Old Party" that fought hard to stop the government expansion during the FDR administration. Unfortunately even back then the infiltration of Progressives into the GOP had begun to transform the party into what it is today. That deep rooted progressive influence has effectively neutered the Republican Party from being a true small-government party.

These reasons, among others, underscore the huge advancement towards freedom a Medina victory would usher in. Here are some of the major gains that would occur:

1. The era of the career politician would be in serious jeopardy. The founders envisioned citizen rule instead of career politicians. Medina's victory coupled with the very likely Rand Paul victory in the Senate race in Kentucky would be huge political statements in support of non-career politicians.

2. Medina's strong 10th amendment platform is exactly the type of philosophy needed to help restore State sovereignty. Texas would become the leader in that cause.

3. Medina is a true tax reformer. Her stand on eliminating the property tax will serve as a blueprint for the rest of the country to end *confiscatory* taxing schemes.

4. Medina's strong 2nd amendment position will help the cause nationally. Recent news reports of Obama's justice department shutting down Gun Shows in Texas underscores the hypocrisy of Rick Perry who has remained silent about the Federal intrusion.

The benefits of a Medina victory would go beyond those

issues mentioned here. The psychological benefits of encouraging frustrated small-government conservatives would have a ripple effect across the country. This is why we advocate Debra Medina's election.

Scott Brown received huge amounts of money from out-of-state. The two Establishment candidates in Texas have a combined total of about 24 million dollars in their war chest. Medina depends on small contributions from grassroots support and can't compete with big corporate donors. Even so Debra Medina has made amazing gains with limited funding and no statewide recognition prior to the first debate.

The second debate Jan 29, 2010, gave her another big bump in the polls and placed her in a legitimate three way race. She is no longer an impossible long shot.

Most of the press in and around Texas has praised her debate performance and acknowledged her elevated status. Debra Medina presents a window of opportunity that rarely presents itself and we as patriots must spread the word about her issues and campaign.

Republican gubernatorial hopeful Debra Medina legally totes a 9 mm pistol (with a 16-round magazine) in a zippered case in her car. But she doesn't want a license to carry it anywhere else.

The Wharton businesswoman favors repealing the Texas concealed handgun law, saying it should not be government's job to license and regulate guns.

This protégé of libertarian-leaning U.S. Rep. Ron Paul is no sheep. She says that decriminalizing marijuana deserves a look. The mother of two home-schooled children, now grown, is also skeptical of the state mandate that children attend public school.

Medina said she voted for Republican George W. Bush for president but not for the GOP's 2008 presidential choice,

U.S. Sen. John McCain, or Democrat Barack Obama.

"That's one of the biggest mistakes Republicans make: Close your eyes, hold your nose and vote for the guy with the 'R' beside his name regardless of what he stands for and what he does," she said.

Making her first race for public office, Medina is chasing well-known, well-funded foes, Gov. Rick Perry and U.S. Sen. Kay Bailey Hutchison.

Barring upheaval, she won't catch them. But she might.

Even so, she could keep one from drawing more than half the March 2 primary vote. She'd then get credit for causing an April runoff, preceded by loads of high-dollar advertising.

Historically, long shots don't win because they're overlooked and ignored. Of late, Medina has complained of being left out of debate plans.

But her fans take heart from 2006, when secession advocate Larry Kilgore drew 7.6 percent of the vote in the GOP gubernatorial primary, and two others together got 8.1 percent, holding Perry to 84%.

Medina hinted that she hopes to overtake Hutchison in the primary before besting Perry in a runoff.

Who knows?

Medina's signature idea — replacing property taxes with sales taxes — might stir voters . . . though the envisioned shift would be a hard sell to legislators.

Analyst Dick Lavine of the Center for Public Policy Priorities estimates the 6.25% state sales tax would need to double to 12.5% to replace the $14 billion in property taxes collected to support public schools and make up for a probable drop in retail spending.

Lavine wonders too how school boards lacking property taxes might raise money.

Medina said boards could ask voters to OK higher sales taxes — a prospect giving districts reason to fight for keeping property taxes.

Medina generally advocates fresh leadership, saying: "There seems to be a lot of slop in state government."

Spoken like a mama, the pistol-packing kind.

5
Debra Medina On Issues
Issues Facing Texas & the United State

Debra on the Role of Government
"That which governs best, governs least"

We Texans understand that our government is made up of the people, by the people, and for the people. The proper role of government is to uphold justice and to prevent *in*justice. Justice is upheld when the natural inalienable rights of man are protected and when government is constrained by the strong bands of our rule of law. We must insure that law applies to one and all the same.

A limited government operating in its proper role allows citizens to reach their full potential thus allowing our state to reach its full potential. Our government should be protecting life, liberty, property, and individual sovereignty. Our government should not be confiscating property, constraining liberties, or making decisions that are better made at the local level by individuals, families, and communities.

Debra on State Sovereignty
"Restore a strong respect for the 10th Amendment"

The Constitution of the United States is a contract between "We the People" to form a limited federal government composed of sovereign states. It creates a republican form of government. Any power not expressly granted to the federal government is reserved for the states and for the people.

Like any party to a contract, Texas must stand up and push back against any attempts to abuse the Constitution or abuse the inalienable rights granted by our Creator.

As individuals, as parents, as families, and as Texans we must be courageous enough to say NO when Washington oversteps its bounds.

We Texans have always believed that the individual and the family are the foundation of America's greatness. We Texans know what's best for our families. We know best how to manage our lives, we know best how to raise our children, and we know best how to spend our money.

By asserting her Constitutional sovereignty, Texas can protect her citizens and provide them the opportunity to succeed. As Governor, I promise to fight back against federal laws that unconstitutionally interfere with the lives of Texans.

Texas can lead. Texas will lead.

Debra on Taxes and Spending

"Cut Taxes + Cut Spending = Reduced Government"

Taxes must be cut, property taxes eliminated, and government spending reduced.

Taxes

"Taxes are the fuel that feeds big government." Taxes are the burden carried by productive citizens. To relieve that burden, taxes must be cut.

Two cornerstones of the American Dream are purchasing a home and starting a business. So why are We Texans punished for pursuing this dream?

As Governor I will fight to end property taxes. This will allow Texans to truly own their piece of Texas. You cannot truly own property that you have to pay the government [ed. rent] for every year.

It's time to remove barriers to opportunity. It's time to start dreaming again in Texas.

Spending

"Reduce spending in order to reduce taxes." The size and scope of government is in direct proportion to the amount that government spends. Size of spending equals

the size of government. Only reduction in spending means less government, less taxes and less intrusion into the lives of responsible Texans. We must cut spending.

As conservatives we all have our favorite federal-level departments we would like to see go, but when have we ever stopped to consider which state-level departments need to go? It is time to return those responsibilities that are better undertaken on the local-level to our counties, our churches and our families.

As Governor I promise to be responsible with the hard-earned money entrusted to Texas by Texans. I promise to work to cut as much spending as possible, so that decisions can be returned to the local-level and the home where they belong and so that more of your money stays in your pocket.

Debra on the Business Climate in Texas
"Remove Barriers to Business in Texas"

The business margins tax, high property taxes, over-regulation, and increased government spending harm the economy and enslave the people. Providing government services at the local level and reducing the spending at the state level will create a magnet for business and strengthen the economy of the state.

As Governor, I will fight to end the business margins tax. This tax is a back-door income tax. This relief will allow businesses to grow. Economic growth leads to more jobs. More jobs lead to a higher standard of living for all Texans.

Debra on Life
"Pro-Life, Period"

Life begins at conception and concludes at natural death.

Every human is created in the image of God. God, not man, is the measure of all things. Every human life is precious and I will work to protect innocent human life.

Debra on Family
"Strong families are the heart and soul of our great

state."

Government must resist interfering in our families. We Texans must support the fundamental rights of parents to determine what is in the best interest of their children. All government policies must be crafted to support the stability of the family and to refrain from undermining it. Government subsidies destroy family bonds, as parents are not required to rely upon one another for support, but instead look towards the nanny state. We must foster individual responsibility, rather than coerce government dependence.

Debra on the Right to Keep and Bear Arms
"No compromise 2nd Amendment"

Gun ownership is essential to our liberty. Private property rights notwithstanding, the right to keep and bear arms should not be regulated or infringed. We Texans should be free to carry our arms openly, and any attempts to restrict gun ownership should be rejected.

Debra on Illegal Immigration
"Illegal Immigration is Illegal"

Illegal immigration affects many aspects of our lives: jobs, health care, education, housing, and taxes to name a few. It also adversely affects the lives of those who come here illegally, as they are forced into an underground culture. Everyone is a victim. The most compassionate thing We Texans can do is stop illegal immigration.

Debra on Education
"Return to Local Control and Expect Excellence"

We Texans deserve excellence in education. We Texans remain concerned about the quality of our schools despite the fact that funding of public education has more than doubled in recent years. Promoting competition, local control, and guidance will allow Texas to reduce cost, increase performance, and improve the quality in our schools.

Our Constitution provides for the support and maintenance of an efficient system of free public schools *"for the general diffusion of knowledge essential to the preservation of the liberties and rights of the people."*

Debra on Healthcare
"Free-Market Healthcare Only"

We Texans should be free to make our own decisions concerning healthcare for our families. Government interference in the medical industry increases medical costs and lowers the quality of healthcare. We must eliminate state mandates and promote a free market for healthcare in order to offer the best medical services to the most people. Families and communities, not government, ought to be allowed and encouraged to provide healthcare to those who need it.

Debra on Private Property
"A Texas truly owned by Texans"

Dominion over ourselves, our private property, and the fruits of our labor is essential to liberty. Property in all its forms must be protected **and property taxes must be eliminated.**

As Governor I will fight state agencies who abuse the power of eminent domain to wrongfully seize property.

"When a portion of wealth is transferred from the person who owns it – without his consent and without compensation, and whether by force or by fraud – to anyone who does not own it, then property is violated and an act of plunder committed" - Frederick Bastiat, The Law.

Debra on The Home
See Chapter 9

This is Woman's Hour

9/11 TRUTHER CONTROVERSY

6
Sarah Palin
On investigating 9/11

Alaska Governor gives unexpected answer re. 9/11 during Ohio rally

October 28, 2008.
Republican vice presidential candidate **Sarah Palin** was asked by **wearechange.org** today if she supports a new 9/11 investigation called for by the victim's family members.

> **Interviewer:** "Will you support the victim's family members and first responders of 9/11, who are calling for a new investigation?"
>
> **Sarah Palin:** "I do, because I think that helps us get to the point of 'never again.' . . . Were you affected?"
>
> **Interviewer:** "Yeah. I have friends that were affected too. I know people. . . . And a lot of them are still sick and dying from the EPA because they lied about the air quality and stuff like that. Thank you for your concern. Thank you so much."

7
Debra Medina
On investigating 9/11

Corporate Media Smears Medina For Expressing View Shared By Majority Of Americans

Friday, February 12, 2010

The attack dog corporate media, in cahoots with phony neo-con Glenn Beck, are once again attempting to manufacture reality by smearing Debra Medina for expressing a view shared by the vast majority of Americans in an effort to purge her from the Texas gubernatorial race.

Fox News performer Glenn Beck attempted to set up Medina on his radio show yesterday by asking her if she believed the U.S. government was involved in 9/11.

"I think some very good questions have been raised in that regard," Medina said. "There are some very good arguments, and I think the American people have not seen all the evidence there, so I have not taken a position on that."

Medina's response was measured and even less vehement that than six of the ten 9/11 commissioners, who have all gone on the record to discuss how the government lied about the official story.

Furthermore, in merely refusing to completely accept the official version of events, Medina stands firmly with the *majority* of Americans. An October 2006 CBS/New York

Times poll found that only 16% of Americans thought the government told the truth about 9/11 and the intelligence prior to the attacks. Medina is in agreement with no less than 84% of Americans who do not readily accept the official story as true.

Callers to 570 KLIF were unanimous in their response to the non-issue, agreeing that Medina's answer was perfectly acceptable, accurate, and that they wouldn't change their vote for her.

The Medina interview is astounding in the fact that it completely unveils how the establishment media has once again brazenly tried, but failed, to dictate reality by claiming that Medina's campaign is now over, despite the fact that the vast majority of Texans **completely agree** with her position on 9/11.

Even so, Medina's statements were immediately seized upon by a political establishment transparently desperate to derail her accelerating poll numbers as she closes in on globalist stooges Rick Perry and Kay Bailey Hutchinson.

All of a sudden, every viewpoint and every opinion of every individual Medina had talked to suddenly became attributed to her as the media aggressively tried to shift the debate away from the issues that have made her so popular in an attempt to tear her down. Beck subsequently expressed his desire to "french kiss" Rick Perry and the fix was in.

Medina has never even talked about 9/11 as part of her state governor's platform, but that didn't stop Hutchinson and Perry operatives flooding Twitter with hoax controversies about her supposed mental instability for daring to say that Americans have the right to question their government.

Within an hour of her appearance on Beck's show, robo-calls from the Perry and Hutchinson campaigns went out attacking Medina as a "9/11 truther".

"Wow!! Isn't that interesting," wrote one respondent to an Austin-American Statesman story. "How was Mr. Perry's team so ready to start a massive robo blitz with this **new Truther news** so quick? Looks like someone is getting scared, and that he had a little help from a friend."

Indeed, for such calls to be launched so soon after Medina's appearance, it's blatant that **Beck's ambush journalism** was carefully planned from the very beginning. Perry and Hutchinson were primed to capitalize upon the fake controversy before it even happened.

But unfortunately for the establishment, it seems like the people are not buying the hoax. Just like the KLIF callers, the majority of respondents to the Statesman story expressed their support for Medina and denounced the **cheap shots** pulled by Glenn Beck.

"Medina raised more than $50,000 yesterday. I doubt that she has "nullified herself". Her popularity is actually **soaring** and Beck is receiving thousands of angry emails," wrote one.

"I just donated $350 to her campaign," added another, pointing out that Medina has never wavered from her campaign which is based on **states' rights, securing the border, gun owners' rights and replacing the unconstitutional property tax** — all issues which both Perry and Hutchinson have completely abandoned in favor of toadying up to the political elite that owns them.

"The real travesty is the hatchet job perpetrated by this reporter and the rest of the pack of corporate owned media running dogs who pose as journalists," added another, highlighting the fact that a candidate in the mould of Medina poses a threat to **both** Democrats and Republicans across the country and the entire two party monopoly that Glenn Beck shills for on a routine basis.

"What Medina said is that there are unanswered questions posed to the government about 911," states another. "This is 100% true and accurate. The 911 Commission's report stated that the government withheld evidence and therefore the report was incomplete with unanswered questions."

For taking a stance similar to six of the ten 9/11 Commissioners, who have all publicly stated that the official story surrounding the attacks is impossible, Medina is being witch hunted by the establishment in a savage McCarthyesque purge.

Medina was gaining on both Perry and Hutchinson at a rate of several points a week. The establishment was straining at the leash to find some mud to sling at her and since they could come up with nothing, they had to engineer a **fake spectacle** by way of the neo-con who poses as a libertarian, Glenn Beck, the man who supported the bailout under Bush and then claimed he had opposed it all along when Obama got in office, the man who ceaselessly calls for more taxes on the American people while posing as a demagogue of the Tea Party movement which is supposed to stand against new taxes.

As little as seven months ago, Rick Perry and John Cornyn were being booed in Texas at Tea Party events. Now Perry has learned to don a cowboy hat and pretend to be a grass roots populist while selling out Texas' very infrastructure to foreign companies that Texans will pay tolls to. The Tea Party movement has been hijacked by phony neo-cons who endorse Perry while the only real Constitutionalist in the race, Debra Medina, is the victim of an organized smear campaign.

Fine, if Republicans want to continue to pay rising property taxes and fees on toll roads to foreign-owned companies, if they want the border to continue to be wide open, then go ahead and vote for Bilderberger Rick Perry — you deserve everything you get.

In the meantime, true Constitutionalists, true conservatives and true patriots will continue to support the people's candidate – Debra Medina – redoubling our efforts in order to expose this entire farce for what it really is — an artificially engineered hatchet job conducted by big government worshipping corporate media pawn – Glenn Beck – the man who proclaims his love for America while selling out every single idea that made America great, the right to dissent, the right to question, and the right to exercise the liberties enshrined in the Constitution and the Bill of Rights, all things that Debra Medina stands for, and all things that Perry and Hutchinson have abandoned.

The Road Ahead

8
9/11 Truth Movement

"9/11 Truth movement" is the collective name of loosely affiliated organizations and individuals who question the mainstream account of the **September 11, 2001 attacks**. Adherents of the movement discuss different hypotheses about how the attacks happened and call for a new investigation into the attacks.

Some of the organizations state that there is evidence that individuals within the **United States government** may have been either responsible for or knowingly complicit in the September 11 attacks. Motives given include the use of the attacks to initiate the launch of **wars in Iraq** and **Afghanistan**, and in creating the opportunities to curtail American **civil liberties**. Members of the movement are often referred to as **"truthers,"** - *"conspiracy theorists,"* occasionally as **"9/11 deniers,"** and by *sympathetic* writers as **"9/11 skeptics."** Members of the movement may hold *diverse* views on other political issues.

Characteristics

"9/11 Truth movement" is the collective name of loosely affiliated organizations and individuals that question whether or not the United States government, agencies of the United States, or individuals within such agencies were either responsible for, or purposefully complicit in the **September 11 attacks**. The term is also being used by the adherents of the movement. Adherents also call themselves "9/11 Truthers," "9/11 skeptics" or "truth activists," while generally rejecting the term "conspiracy theorists".

Adherents of the 9/11 Truth movement come from diverse social backgrounds. The movement draws adherents from both the left and the right. The Conservative supporters of the movement often come from a Libertarian background.

Prominent adherents of the movement include, among many others, theologian **David Ray Griffin**, physicist **Steven E. Jones**, software engineer **Jim Hoffman**, architect **Richard Gage**, film producer **Dylan Avery**, former member of the U.S. House of Representatives **Cynthia McKinney**, actors **Daniel Sunjata**, **Ed Asner**, and **Charlie Sheen**, political science professor **Joseph Diaferia** and journalists **Thierry Meyssan** and **Robert Fisk**.

According to Lev Grossman of *TIME magazine*, support for the 9/11 Truth movement is not a "fringe phenomenon" but "a mainstream political reality." Mark Fenster, a **University of Florida** law professor and author of the book *Conspiracy Theories: Secrecy and Power in American Culture*, says that "the amount of organization" of the movement is significantly stronger than the organization of the movement related to doubts about the official account of the assassination of former United States President **John F. Kennedy**, though this is likely the result of **new media** technologies, such as online **social networks**, **blogs**, etc.

See also: **9/11 conspiracy theories**.

Many adherents of the 9/11 Truth movement suspect that United States government insiders played a part in the attacks, or at the very least knew they were coming and let them occur anyway.

Those within the movement who argue that insiders within the United States government were directly responsible for the September 11 attacks often allege that the attacks were planned and executed in order to provide the U.S. with a pretext for going to war in the Middle East and, by extension, as a means of consolidating and extending the power of the Bush Administration and the New World Order.

According to these allegations, this would have given the Bush administration the justification to clamp down on civil liberties and invade Iraq and Afghanistan to ensure future supplies of oil. In some cases, hawks in **the White House**, especially former Vice President **Dick Cheney**, and members of the ***Project for the New American Century***, a neoconservative think tank, have been accused of involvement in or awareness of the alleged plot.

Many adherents of the 9/11 Truth movement allege that the buildings of the World Trade Center had been destroyed by **controlled demolition**, a theory of major importance for the 9/11 Truth movement.

The Internet plays a large role both in the communication between adherents and between local groups of the 9/11 Truth movement and in the dissemination of the views of the movement to the public at large.

Both before and after the **9/11 Commission Report**, there were skeptics of the official account published by the Bush Administration. Among others, Michael Ruppert and Canadian journalist **Barrie Zwicker**, published criticisms or pointed out purported anomalies of the mainstream account of the attacks. **French** author **Jean-Charles Brisard** and **German** authors **Mathias Bröckers** and **Andreas von Bülow** published books critical of media reporting and advancing the controlled demolition thesis of the destruction of the World Trade Center towers.

In September 2002, the first **"Bush Did It!"** rallies and

marches were held in **San Francisco** and **Oakland, California** organized by The All People's Coalition.

In October 2004, the organization *9/11 Truth* released a statement, signed by nearly 200 people, including many relatives of people who perished on September 11, 2001, that calls for an investigation into the attacks. It also asserted that unanswered questions would suggest that people within the administration of former President **G. W. Bush** may have deliberately allowed the attacks to happen. Actor **Edward Asner**, former presidential candidate **Ralph Nade**r, former congresswoman **Cynthia McKinney**, former assistant secretary of housing **Catherine Austin Fitts**, author **Richard Heinberg**, **Enver Masud**, founder of **The Wisdom Fund**, professors **Richard Falk** of the University of California, **Mark Crispin Miller** of New York University, **Douglas Sturm** of Bucknell University, **Burns H. Weston** of the Iowa Law School and others signed the statement. In 2009, **Van Jones**, a former advisor to President Obama, said he hadn't fully reviewed the statement before he signed and that the petition did not reflect his views "now or ever."

In 2006, **Steven E. Jones**, who became a leading academic voice of the demolition theory, published the paper "Why Indeed Did the WTC Buildings Completely Collapse?". He was placed on paid leave by **Brigham Young University** following what they described as Jones's "increasingly speculative and accusatory" statements in September, 2006, pending a review of his statements and research. Six weeks later, Jones retired from the university.

In the same year, 61 legislators in the U.S. State of Wisconsin signed a petition calling for the dismissal of a **University of Wisconsin** assistant professor **Kevin**

Barrett, after he joined the group *Scholars for 9/11 Truth*. Citing **academic freedom**, the university **provost** declined to take action against Barrett.

Several organizations of family members of people who have died in the attacks are calling for an independent investigation into the attacks. In 2009, a group of people, including 9/11 Truth movement activist **Lorie Van Auken** and others who have lost friends or relatives in the attack, appealed to the City of New York to investigate the disaster. The organization *New York City Coalition for Accountability Now* is collecting signatures to require the New York City Council to place the creation of an investigating commission on the November 2009 election ballot.

9/11 Commission Report reaction

To the consternation of the families and adherents of the 9/11 Truth movement, many of the questions that the **9/11 Family Steering Committee** put to the **9/11 Commission**, chaired by former **New Jersey** Governor **Thomas Kean**, were not asked in either the hearings or in the Commission Report. **Lorie Van Auken**, one of the **Jersey Girls**, estimates that only 30% of their questions were answered in the final 9/11 Commission Report, published July 22, 2004. The story of the Families Movement and their monitoring of the commission is documented in the film *9/11: Press for Truth* (2006).

The **9/11 Family Steering Committee** produced a website summarizing the questions they had raised to the Commission, indicating which they believe had been answered satisfactorily, which they believe had been addressed but not answered satisfactorily, and which they believe had been generally ignored in, or omitted from the Report.

In addition, the 339-page book *The 9/11 Commission*

Report: Omissions and Distortions by **David Ray Griffin**, claimed that the report had either omitted information or distorted the truth, providing 115 alleged examples. He has characterized the 9/11 Commission Report as "a 571-page lie".

On May 26, 2008 college professor **Blair Gadsby** began a protest and a hunger strike outside the offices of **Senator** and **Republican Party** Nominee for President **John McCain**'s office demanding to see John McCain. Arizona Republican State Senator **Karen Johnson** joined the protest in support. On June 10 Johnson with Gadsby as her guest and other 9/11 Truth movement members in the audience spoke before the **Arizona State Senate** espousing the **controlled demolition theory** and supporting a reopening of the 9/11 investigation. In response to a question, McCain, who wrote the foreword to a book published by the magazine *Popular Mechanics*, that aims at debunking the theories, said he did not meet Gadsby, adding: "Because I don't take well to threats."

NIST Report reaction

An Iron-rich *sphere* was found in the dust of the World Trade Center, as documented by the United States Geological Survey. According to **Steven Jones**, NIST did not look for evidence of explosive residue.

Following the initial government investigation, the **Federal Emergency Management Agency** (FEMA) Report (May 2002) **NIST Report**, numerous responses were written by members of the 9/11 Truth movement. Many of these responses claimed that it ignored key evidence suggesting an explosive demolition, "distorted reality" by using deceptive language and diagrams, and attacked **strawman** arguments, such as the 2005 article by **Jim Hoffman** entitled, *Building a better mirage: NIST's 3-year $20,000,000 Cover Up of the Crime of the Century*.

In the fall of 2005, **Steven Jones**, a professor at **Brigham Young University** at the time, announced a paper criticizing the NIST Report and describing his hypothesis that the WTC towers had been intentionally demolished by explosives. This paper garnered some mainstream media attention, including an appearance by Jones on **MSNBC**. This was the first such programming on a major cable news station. As of September 2009, Jones had not published his research in peer-reviewed mainstream journals. Jones was criticized by his university for making his claims public before vetting them through the approved peer review process. He was placed on paid leave and has since retired. He continues to remain a focus of public interest for his 9/11 research.

Accordingly, in April 2007, some 9/11 victims' family members and some members of the new **Scholars for 9/11 Truth and Justice** submitted an additional request for correction to NIST, containing their own views on the defects in the report. NIST responded to this request in September 2007 supporting their original conclusions; the originators of the request wrote back to them in October 2007, asking them to reconsider their response.

Criticism

In 2006, a book critic with *Time* magazine noted that a major problem with films such as **Loose Change** and most 9/11 conspiracy theories in general is that [ed. allegedly] "the more one thinks about them, the more one realizes how much they depend on circumstantial evidence, facts without analysis, quotes taken out of context, and the scattered testimony of traumatized eyewitnesses". **Matt Taibbi** of ***Rolling Stone*** assessed that the movement "gives supporters of **Bush** an excuse to dismiss critics of this administration" and expressed concerns about the number of people who believe in 9/11 conspiracy theories.

Noam Chomsky stated that, regarding US government involvement in the 9/11 attacks, "the evidence that has been produced is essentially worthless" and while the American government stood to benefit from the incident, "every authoritarian system in the world gained from September 11th." He argues that the enormous risk of an information **leak**, "it is a very porous system and secrets are very hard to keep", and consequences of exposure for the Republican party would have made such a conspiracy foolish to attempt. He dismisses observations cited by conspiracy proponents saying, "if you look at the evidence, anybody who knows anything about the sciences would instantly discount that evidence," arguing that even when a scientific experiment is carried out repeatedly in a controlled environment, phenomena and coincidences remain that are unexplained.

MIT engineering professor **Thomas W. Eagar** was at first unwilling to acknowledge the concerns of the movement, saying "if (the argument) gets too mainstream, I'll engage in the debate." In response to **Steven E. Jones** publishing a hypothesis that the World Trade Center was destroyed by controlled demolition, **Eager** said that adherents of the 9/11 Truth movement would use the ***reverse scientific method*** to arrive at their conclusions, as they "determine what happened, throw out all the data that doesn't fit their conclusion, and then hail their findings as the only possible conclusion.

Former President **Bill Clinton** dismissed 9/11 conspiracy

theories saying "Nine-eleven was NOT an inside job, it was an Osama Bin Laden job with 19 people from Saudi Arabia, they murdered 3000 Americans and others; foreigners including Muslims."

The Road Ahead

Debra Medina On The Home

9
The Home

From time immemorial the home has been the most important factor in human society. It is at once the cradle of civilization, the foundation of society, and the cement that binds and holds them together.

The highest ideal, the chief ambition of good American citizens, young or old, is to own their own home. The home is a man's castle. It should be inviolate from all intrusion. It should be placed beyond the reach of all danger, and of every encroachment, whether of private or public origin. It should be exempt from attachment. Not even the government should be permitted to take a man's home away from him.

No nation rises above the conditions of the nation's homes. Destroy the home, and by that act you at the same time destroy the nation.

Because of unemployment, thousands of workers are daily loosing their homes through foreclosures of mortgages, and execution for debt and tax sales. And yet nothing is done to prevent this wholesale destruction of the chief asset of the nation.

Is it more important to declare a moratorium on foreign debts or bailouts for the banks than it is to protect the homes of the nation's people by a similar relief?

For shame on our great humanitarian leaders who rant and rail about balancing budgets that they cannot even budge, let alone balance; and can find no better way to get out of the dilemma that they, themselves, have precipitated than to purloin additional taxes through bailouts that can but sink the helpless taxpayer deeper in the treacherous quicksands of shifting usury and taxation.

Just where is this insane policy ultimately leading us? We have allowed the government to tax us, and that power, mind you, is the power to destroy.

We look to the government to protect us, and suddenly we find the government oppressing us. This is nobody's fault but our own, for we are the government. If we permit it to run wild and pile up unconscionable expenses, we may expect that it will tax us to pay its unreasonable bills.

But the time has come to call a halt to this policy. We cannot permit the government to eat up our homes.

Foreclosures help no one, not even the lenders themselves, who, in most cases, not only find themselves with an unproductive piece of property on their hands, but are confronted with the immediate necessity for additional expenditures for much needed repairs and improvements, and the payment of delinquent taxes that have perhaps accumulated against this property, considerably under the sum for which they were bid in.

And yet, more than two millions farms alone have been taken away thusly from their helpless owners in recent years. One insurance company alone has thus reportedly foreclosed on more than one million acres of the best farm lands in Illinois and it is reported that one large banking institution on the Pacific Coast has more that 7,000 ranches on its hands which it has acquired by similar tactics. Is it any wonder that the value of its stock is about one percent of what it was before it started on this rampage of wholesale foreclosures?

The banks, the Insurance Companies, the Building and Loan Associations and Mortgage and Trust Companies were loaded to the point of breaking with farm mortgages and mortgages on homes and other buildings, before the bailouts. These mortgages constituted some of the 'frozen assets' that banks had so recently unloaded upon the long-suffering and indignant tax-payer.

What irony; what an insult to our intelligence! We permit the government to increase taxes to the point of confiscation. We permit these private interests to deflate the currency and restrict the credit of the nation until the value of the dollar is driven up and the value of our products is driven down, to the point where production costs far exceed the sale prices of our products; then when these same private interests require us to pay a dollar obligation with a ten cent bushel of wheat, and our land will not produce the required number of bushels of ten cent wheat to pay the dollar mortgage, we allow these same private interests to foreclose on our lands and deprive us of our homes. And as a *final* insult to our intelligence we permit the government to add insult to injury by advancing these same private institutions money which we will again repay through taxation.

If, by protecting the home, whether in city, town or country, we strike at the very heart of disloyalty and discontent, then why is this not the most important thing for our lawmakers to consider, in lieu of bailing out the banks?

What avails it if we declare a moratorium on national debts to relieve European nations from us, their creditors, if we, at the same time, permit the spectre of unemployment and poverty, low prices, and foreclosures to destroy the nation from domestic enemies within.

We urge upon our government, first, to declare a moratorium on debts that jeopardize the home, whether in city, town or country, pending the present depression; second, to take definite steps, through the extension of the Homestead Act, to gradually, but permanently, make the home, whether in city, town, or country, forever 'tax exempt and execution free!'

This is not an unreasonable or revolutionary undertaking. It may be brought about in an orderly manner that will hurt no one. The benefits to be derived from such a program would be legion.

Home and farm mortgages have from time immemorial, been considered the safest investments on earth. Could any security be devised that would even approach, from the standpoint of moral risk and physical value, the security that is offered by a farm or home loan? Can it be successfully argued that the notes of a private banking institutions, even when backed by the guarantee of the Government, which in itself has been shown to be in large measure dependent upon the security of its home owners, is superior to the security offered by the home?

Then why should the government not issue 'interest amortizing free currency' in sufficient quantity to absorb all the farm and home mortgages now in the hands of the Banks, Insurance Companies, Building and Loan Associations and other similar financial institutions that, before being bailed out, were breaking under the strain for 'frozen assets' in the form of farm and home mortgages?

Such a course would have been a decided advantage to everyone.

The finance houses would have exchanged their frozen assets for 'interest amortizing free currency' instead of credit debt borrowed at interest from the non-federal Federal Reserve Bank, in the place of the mortgages that jeopardized their very existence.

The Government could have then refinanced these short term mortgages that it would have been holding in consideration for the issuance of its 'interest amortizing free currency' into new loans running for from 30 to 50 years similar to those now made by the Federal Land Bank, the only Simon-pure, co-operative, borrower-owned financial institution in America outside the realm of a few mutual Building and Loan Associations that have managed to escape the trap laid for them by the nefarious methods and legislation prompted by the special privilege and crooked building and loan officials.

Such a course would confiscate no man's property, it would summarily stop foreclosures, and the attendant ruinous loss to creditor and debtor alike. It would check the downward turn of reality values due to foreclosures. It would put back into circulation several billions of dollars that had been squeezed out of circulation by that hideous monster, the non-federal Federal Reserve Bank, and it would have automatically balanced the budget which we hear so much about by adding a billions or so to our national income from the 'interest amortizing free currency' thus put into circulation.

We don't hear you, Mr. Banker.

The tragic wails of a hundred million destitute, poverty stricken, hungry, hopeless human beings submerge into utter oblivion the most frantic protests you are able to muster from the comparative handful of human barnacles that threaten to sink our majestic ship of State. Neither do we hear the feeble peep of legislators who have a 'committee appointed for the purpose' of determining the policies best adapted to fit the currency needs of the nation, and thus seek to avoid the responsibility of their office.

BORN AGAIN, AMERICAN

WATCH THE VIDEO

http://tinyurl.com/bwnqtv

This is Woman's Hour

BORN AGAIN, AMERICAN

I'm just a workin' man without a job,
   It got shipped off to China, via Washington D.C.
And I know I'm nothin' special, there are plenty more like me,
but just the same,
   I thought I knew the rules of the game

I stood up for this country that I love,
   I came back from the desert, to a wife and kids to feed
I'm not sayin' Uncle Sam should give me what I need,
my offer stands,
   I'll pull my weight 'you give me half a chance

And I went up to a congressman, and said to him, "You know
   Our government is letting people down."
He said he'd need a lot of help to buck the status quo
   I said there was a bunch of us around

I'm a Born, Again, American,
   Conceived in liberty
My Bible and the Bill of Rights
   My creed's equality
I'm a Born, Again, American
   My country 'tis of me
And every-one who shares the dream
   From sea to shining sea.

My brother's welding chassis at the plant
   He's earning what our gran-dad did in nineteen forty-eight
While CEOs count bonuses behind the castle gates
   How can they see, If all they care about's the do-re-me

It's getting where there's nowhere left to turn,
   Not since the crash of twenty-nine have things been so unfair
So many of our citizens are living in despair,
   The time has come, to reaffirm that hope's not just for some

The promise of America's surrendering to greed
  The rule is just look out for number one,
But brace yourself 'cause some of us have sown a different seed,
  A harvest of the spirit has begun.

II'm a Born, Again, American,
  Conceived in liberty
My Bible and the Bill of Rights
  My creed's equality
I'm a Born, Again, American
  My country 'tis of me
And every-one who shares the dream
  From sea to shining sea.

It's clear my country's soul is on the line,
  She's hungering for something that she's lost along the way,
The principle the Framers called upon us to obey, That is this land,
  The people's Will must have the upper hand

I felt the call, as once before, and took a sacred vow
  And faithful to that vow I have remained,
I hear the call that once again my country needs me now
  I hear her call I have been re-ordained

I'm a Born, Again, American,
  Conceived in liberty
My Bible and the Bill of Rights
  My creed's equality
I'm a Born, Again, American
  My country 'tis of me
And every-one who shares the dream
  From sea to shining sea.

And every-one who shares the dream,
  From sea . . . to shining sea
    America, . . America!

"My God shall supply all your need according to his riches in glory by Christ Jesus." — *Phillipians 4:19*

Oil Benearh Our Feet: *America's Energy Non-crisis*
http://tinyurl.com/ya58fwq

Commercial Redemption: *The Hidden Truth*
http://tinyurl.com/yj4otn4

Untold History Of America: *Let The Truth Be Told*
http://tinyurl.com/y8hwvzr

New Beginning Study Course: *Connect The Dots And See*
http://tinyurl.com/ybxdvgp

Monitions of a Mountain Man: *Manna, Money, & Me*
http://tinyurl.com/ygtkak8

Maine Street Miracle: *Saving Yourself And America*
http://tinyurl.com/yg9q8mm

Reclaim Your Sovereignty: *Take Back Your Christian Name*
http://tinyurl.com/y8kuutb

Epistle to the Americans I: *What you don't know about The Income Tax*
http://tinyurl.com/yfplutf

Epistle to the Americans II: *What you don't know about American History*
http://tinyurl.com/yzme458

Epistle to the Americans III: *What you don't know about Money*
http://tinyurl.com/yzuffbe